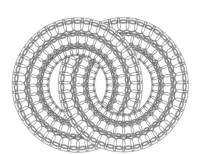

History Is Embarrassing

History Is Embarrassing

Essays

Karen Chase

CAVANKERRY
PRESS

CavanKerry Press Ltd.
Fort Lee, New Jersey
www.cavankerrypress.org

Publisher's Cataloging-in-Publication Data
provided by Five Rainbows Cataloging Services
Names: Chase, Karen, 1943- author.
Title: History is embarrassing : essays / Karen Chase.
Description: Fort Lee, NJ : CavanKerry Press, 2024.
Identifiers: ISBN 978-1-960327-02-4 (paperback) | ISBN 978-1-960327-03-1 (ebook)
Subjects: LCSH: Essays—21st century. | Autobiography. | Poliomyelitis—Vaccination.
| Psychiatric hospital care. | Mothers and sons. |Roosevelt, Franklin D. (Franklin Delano), 1882-1945. | BISAC: BIOGRAPHY & AUTOBIOGRAPHY / Personal Memoirs. | BIOGRAPHY & AUTOBIOGRAPHY / Women.
Classification: LCC RC489.P6 C453 2024 (print) | LCC RC489.P6 C453 2024 (ebook)
| DDC 616.89/165—dc23.

Cover Artwork by Matthew Chase-Daniel & Mayfly Design
Cover and interior text design by Mike Corrao, Mayfly Design
First Edition 2024, Printed in the United States of America

 Made possible by funds from the
New Jersey State Council on the Arts, a partner
agency of the National Endowment for the Arts.

CavanKerry Press is grateful for the support it receives from the New Jersey State Council on the Arts.

In addition, CavanKerry Press gratefully acknowledges generous emergency support received during the COVID-19 pandemic from the following funders:

The Academy of American Poets
Community of Literary Magazines and Presses
National Book Foundation
New Jersey Arts and Culture Recovery Fund
New Jersey Council for the Humanities
New Jersey Economic Development Authority
Northern New Jersey Community Foundation
The Poetry Foundation
US Small Business Administration

Contents

Preface

George Orwell wrote an essay called "Why I Write." Joan Didion stole his title for one of hers. She said that that the words "Why I Write" sounded to her like *I I I*. That's what I'm stealing.

The personal essays in this volume are really personal. The stories are all about me and my life. This is embarrassing because it shows how self-centered a person can be. What's not embarrassing is that this is a book about history. Because each one of us is one tiny dot in the enormous flow and flood of humans from the beginning until now. Whether your dot is large or small—it doesn't matter—each life is equally a story that adds to the human story. This is what comprises history. *E pluribus unum*. History is embarrassing because like it or not, you my reader, whether you are a clerk or a king, you are part of history. Say your name out loud. That name is part of history.

This volume is both a collection of odds and ends and something more. It weaves together the threads from one single life that begins in the twentieth century and will end in the twenty-first century. It tells how this particular person moved forward at this particular time on earth—what befell her, the work she did, her family. Her childhood polio placed her smack in the middle of an historic plague, placing her in history.

The characters in almost all the essays are outsiders. Undercover cops, poets, homosexuals, bear poachers, psychiatric patients, even a president. FDR's polio turned him into an outsider which affected how he saw the world. As a girl with polio, as a poet, a Jew, a writer, and a painter, I am an outsider too. Come join us in the following pages.

One:

Histories

BOOM

A Vaccine Story

Winter is approaching. The garage guys are putting snow tires on my car, so I have to kill some time. Because of the fierce wind, I find shelter at Subway and order a tuna sandwich. After that, I take cover in the Post Road Junk Store. On a shelf, I notice a book filled with matchbooks. Scraps of bright color and word, page after page of actual matchbooks, concrete little squares of history. History looms small and large all at once. Strike a match for history.

One matchbook advertises War Bonds, one for Waldorf Cafeterias, one for RCA Victor. There's one for *Sunset Boulevard,* for Playland at the Beach, for Orange Crush, Mighty Mouse, and one for Hotel Roosevelt. And then, there's

JOIN THE MARCH OF DIMES

HELP

Fight Infantile Paralysis

NOW

SEND DIMES TO YOUR PRESIDENT

The president was Franklin Delano Roosevelt, himself a survivor of infantile paralysis, also known as polio. It was 1938. Radio appeals began. A few days later, truckloads of dimes kept pulling up to 1600 Pennsylvania Avenue. People's enthusiasm made them inventive. They sent dimes "baked into cakes, jammed into cans, imbedded in wax, and glued into profiles of the President." The White House was drowning in dimes. "The government of the United States darned near stopped functioning," said the head of the mailroom.

In a state of delight, FDR sat around smoking cigarettes, watching mountains of coins accumulate. In the first appeal, 2,680,000 dimes were received.

Twelve years later and still no cure. It was summertime 1950, the threatening season. Polio terrified the country, killing and crippling at random. It lurked anywhere, came on as easily as a cold. Any fever, stiff neck, or sore throat caused hysteria. My local newspaper reported how my little friends and I helped the national effort.

POLIO BENEFIT

Larchmont police today are in possession of an envelope containing $3.08, which was delivered to them yesterday afternoon by seven girls, all approximately seven years old, who asked that the money be turned over to the March of Dimes.

They revealed that the money represented the proceeds of a puppet show which they had conducted and that they wanted to give it to help less fortunate children.

1953. I was a sprouting ten-year-old girl, and all was well. I'd hop on my bike and help my older brother deliver newspapers up and down the streets of our town. I'd swim in the Long Island Sound, a short bike ride from our house. And I had a new baby sister! I was in fifth grade. One day while I was walking home from school for lunch, kicking a stone down the road, my legs began to hurt.

After a peanut butter and jelly sandwich and glass of cold milk, I said, "Mom, I can't go back to school today." My neck got stiff, my fever rose alarmingly, and what started as small pains turned into large ones. The doctor came and soon I was rushed to the hospital in an ambulance.

Everyone knew someone who got polio in the 1950s—somebody's cousin, somebody's best friend, someone's neighbor, a classmate, a sister. Polio scared everyone. Parents, grandparents, cousins, uncles, aunts—families were terrified of polio. Schools were, camps were—pick any group and they were terrified. Nieces got polio, nephews got it, cousins got it, a family friend, a kid on your block, a kid in your class, one you liked, one you didn't like, and there they were, paralyzed. Braces, crutches, wheelchairs, or dead.

The fear of polio that swept across the country was not new. Numerous polio epidemics had broken out in the twentieth century. The summer of 1916 saw one of the worst. A newspaper reported, "Panic froze the East, particularly New York City where 2,000 died and another 7,000 were attacked, three-fourths of them children under five. Thousands tried to leave—police at highways and railroad stations halted them. Few hospitals would take polio cases. Police had to break into apartments to take dead children from their mothers."

⟪⟫

A few months after I am rushed to the hospital, I'm a patient in Sunshine Cottage, the hospital polio ward. Hot packs this afternoon. They take hot blankets out of a steaming machine, roll me up in them, wrap me tight until I cool down. Later Mac is coming to have me do leg lifts, arm lifts, and then I can't wait until Mom comes. I wonder what it's like at home. It's hard to even remember my baby sister, Maggi. She must be so big now. I can't even think what she looks like. I get so homesick. I try not to cry, but sometimes I can't help it. It's almost lunchtime. There's snow outside. A letter from my last year's teacher just arrived and it makes me laugh.

I have been teaching my kids about atomic energy. Some of the boys think they know so much about it, they are going to try to make an A bomb. You'll know they were successful if you hear a loud boom.

Boom. Dennis and Jeff and I are playing Monopoly. I have hotels on Marvin Gardens and Atlantic. I'm on a stretcher, Jeff's in his wheelchair, and Dennis sits on a regular chair. The radio is on. Wait, wait—what's this? Someone on the radio is saying that Dr. Somebody made a vaccine from monkeys—from rhesus monkeys. Dr. Jonas Salk minced up tissues from monkeys' kidneys and put them in test tubes with . . . what? People won't get polio anymore! Dennis and I start to laugh. We are laughing so hard that a nurse comes over. Jeff is quiet.

I say, "Monkey kidney, monkey kidney," and we start up again laughing hysterically.

Then Dennis says, "A little late."

Since Jonas Salk's scientific discovery, his vaccine has saved the lives and well-being of millions of people all over the world. In fact, various vaccines have saved many millions of lives during the past two hundred years or so, starting with the smallpox vaccine. Sadly, there have always been vaccine doubters. This holds true today in the shadow of the Covid-19 pandemic, which has killed many millions of people. *Boom.*

Polio Boulevard

Everything leads me back to my polio days now. Last week I drove to a used bookstore on back roads to pick up a biography of Jonas Salk. I noticed a junky antique store, pulled over, puttered through. An old piece of furniture was chained to the store's side porch—a hospital bed from upstate, where there had been a tuberculosis sanatorium long ago. It was oak and painted a darkish green. The works that made it go up and down were cast-iron, and they were painted green too. The springs were spiraling. I fell in love with the bed and bought it.

The next morning, Memorial Day, I woke at six to meet the fellow who delivered the bed in his pickup. He unloaded it, I gave him a check, he left. I dragged the hose out, filled a pail with soapy water, scrubbed the thing down, and let it dry in the rising sun. The foam mattress in the basement just fit. I put a rose-colored sheet on it and dragged the bed under the maple tree. The day was just beginning.

Lying on this not-just-any bed brings me back to how full of motion the world was as I watched it from my polio bed. Everything but me seemed to be moving. I was immobilized in New York, high up on a hospital ward overlooking the East River. I was horizontal, covered in plaster, couldn't get out of bed, couldn't sit, couldn't walk. I was flat. I had a view of the river and what I did was watch.

I watched boats pass from morning to night. I watched smoke billowing out of huge smokestacks, cars heading south on FDR

Drive, cars heading north, a helicopter flying across the sky, a jet carving a diagonal line across the blue as it took off from LaGuardia, boats moving, water moving. I watched the river's current.

One day I was looking out the window when a submarine surfaced right in front of the hospital. It was sunny, I'm sure of it, and slowly the sub rose from the water. A bunch of uniformed sailors appeared on deck. Airy and light, it was the sight of victory.

From my bed, I would look out the window across the river to Queens as morning came. It would be barely dark. A light bulb would go on in a window and cast a sweet orange gleam—artificial, antiquated. I'd wonder about the person who turned the light on—why were they getting up so early, where were they going? I always had them going. They'd be going and I'd be watching.

～～～

It's taken me decades to walk over to my desk, sit down once and for all, and write about what happened when I was a ten-year-old girl with polio.

Here I go . . . It's November . . . It's 1953 . . . My family is living in the well-to-do village of Larchmont, New York, on Long Island Sound . . . I'm in fifth grade . . .

For lunch Mom makes me a peanut butter and jelly sandwich cut in the shape of a house. When I'm done, instead of heading back to school, I go lie down on the bed in the TV room.

I'm resting, which I never do. I don't even feel like watching TV. Look. There's one leg up in the air. My leg—I keep looking at it—I like looking at it. Maybe it hurts. Maybe it feels rusty or something. I'll say it hurts and maybe I can stay home this afternoon. I don't want to give that book report.

My knees are skinned. When I was little, I used to sneak down near the beach with Jimmy Keenan. We liked to climb up on the roof of an old brick garage, jump off onto the ground. Sometimes my knees got scraped and my legs got bruised.

I like my legs. I don't know why. They're just legs, but *just legs* is great. I like the bones of them, how they join. Some people talk about legs that are particularly long. My mother's are particularly bony. Mine aren't particularly anything.

I just swallowed—*I noticed* I swallowed. Just did it again. The back of my throat feels small and getting smaller.

I looked at the clock a few minutes ago. Now I look at it again, but the minute hand has hardly moved. I can hear my baby sister fooling around outside.

I better get up—I've got to start back to school. Today is going so slowly. I wait for minutes to pass. Look at the clock. Ow ow ow—my leg does kind of hurt. But after school, Patsy and I are going to bike to Flint Park.

It's the next day. The doctor comes into my room. He helps me sit on the edge of my bed. He opens his black bag, takes out a rubber mallet. Tap. He taps my knee. My leg does not move.

My mother and I are together, traveling fast in an ambulance. Her hazel eyes are open wide, her face tight. Feverish, I am looking out the window. A breeze moves the highest limbs of a maple. A bird parts the air.

I'm burning up. When we zoom past school, I look at the whizzing brick wall and think *book report,* and then I don't think anything.

The ambulance pulls up to a hospital. Men slide me fast out the back of it. My father, who has followed the ambulance in our car, is standing with my mother. They're like large guards, unmoving. The men slide me around on the ambulance stretcher. My body is frozen. The earth, earthquake-like, is shaking.

"Karen," my father tells me later, "your mother's hair turned white that year."

Soon, hot and tiny, I'm swimming in a sea. There is water and me, and me swimming hard as I can in a blackening bigness. My solid parents are an enlarging wooden raft.

I am attached to something crazy, some crazy transportation. The ambulance stretcher? No, the rush of the iron lung, which helps me breathe. The iron lung is an ivory-enameled metal tube with chrome portholes, and rests steady on the wooden ward floor. All my limbs are concealed. My head, separated from the rest of me on a slanted headrest, sticks out. I cannot move my head or anything at all.

The iron lung is my magic boat, a boat for one. A rhythm boat— in out, in out, in out. The portholes suggest foreign places. My body is inside the iron lung, but my mind is outside. I'm traveling.

⁂

Suddenly I see my dreamboat in a black bathrobe. He's walking to a podium. He's gripping the podium with his strong hands. He has spent years perfecting the illusion of walking. No, it's not my father, it's somebody else! Now he's leaning against the podium. *Leaning,* that's the main thing.

FDR's black robe billows out. His strong-boned face looks polished, like a stone memorial.

A thread of balance holds him up. When the wind blows, maybe he'll fall. Exposed are heavy black steel braces encasing his withered legs. He has just returned from Marrakech. There he was carried up a mountain to see the sun set. Next thing, daylight.

⁂

Now I dream I'm anybody in the audience, watching newsreels. A man in black trousers and black hat is addressing Congress. His shiny braces are outside his pants. He no longer conceals them. I swear, he's wearing gold lamé shoes! I can't breathe.

I wake up, can't fall back to sleep, and start to count. Soon after a thousand, I switch to sound—*va va voom. Va va voom,* I repeat, but remain alert. Then *va voom* works and finally I sleep.

Another newsreel. The man is wheeling around a racetrack on a maroon-tufted armchair. The gong goes off. His chair speeds around the course, he has a rust-colored leg on his lap, and a blue enameled axe. The wind swirling in the distance has a stormy smell.

One birch bends down at the edge of the screen, heavy with spring snow. Wind lifts up the armchair. Stars mix together in the purple sky, then flop in a heap to the ground.

Now in the casbah, FDR is relaxing, drinking vodka with Winston Churchill late at night. What's a casbah? Smoking a cigar, he puffs smoke rings into the air, watches them disappear. There's nothing to fear, he says as wind blows and buries the casbah in sand.

A silky sash around his steel waist holds closed his coral wool coat, like one my grandmother made for me when I was little and could run really fast. His feet are clad in bandaged white boots. The newsreel stops.

The sky lightens, the air is washed—it's never been so full of promise, so clear, so new, as if there had never been a war.

Out in the bristling air, Roosevelt and I are perambulating together, citizens of this great land.

⋘⋙

One morning in August 1921, Franklin Delano Roosevelt, a young politician, noticed a forest fire while sailing in the Bay of Fundy. He was not yet the governor of New York, not yet the president of the United States of America. He and his children rushed ashore and broke off pine branches to fight the flames. By the end of the afternoon, exhausted, they returned to Campobello, their summer home. They jogged across the island and swam in a freshwater lagoon. Then, for "refreshment," FDR went for a quick dip in the freezing bay.

He was "too tired to dress" by the time he got home, and sat in his wet bathing suit, reading mail. "I didn't feel the usual reaction, the glow I'd expected," he said later. Chilled, he walked up the stairs without supper.

The next morning, "when I swung out of bed, my left leg lagged, but I managed to move about to shave. I tried to persuade myself that the trouble with my leg was muscular. . . . But presently it refused to work, and then the other."

Roosevelt never walked again.

History is embarrassing. It's embarrassing to be part of history. My life is small, history is big, best to stay small. You can hold the matchbooks of history in your hand.

My life is small, your life is small, my town is small and always was. If you don't make the connections, you can stay small, but all in all, history is big. And so are you and so am I because we're people and we're alive.

It's embarrassing to write about yourself because of what my mother said. Best to be a lady, private and dignified. But she did give me a great fountain pen with a fat point. Was it her way of urging me to be bold?

For Roosevelt, anything less than history was embarrassing. History was him and he would make it and what a job he would do. He was a patrician and I'm from peasant Ashkenazi stock. He was a man and I was a girl.

The late, great actor Orson Welles is looking at the president of the United States. FDR is saying, "Orson, you and I are the two best actors in America." His braces painted black, he wears black

12

pants cut long, black socks, and shoes. Believing it is political suicide to look crippled, he employs camouflage and illusion.

"He developed this technique that looked like walking . . . . he would lean on one son's arm, putting all his weight on it, and then he would switch his weight from the son's arm onto a cane which he carried in the other hand so that he could switch his weight from side to side and thus progress," reported the writer Hugh Gallagher.

"He instructed his sons, 'You must not let people see that this is difficult or takes effort or it hurts.' They would chat and joke and laugh as they went along . . . . they looked as though they were taking their time so they could smile at people and say hello to the crowd . . . . It was show biz, but it worked."

He is carried to his place at the White House dinner table before guests arrive. The public never sees this. He detests it, but he is carried all over.

꧁꧂

I'm stuck in bed, in this hospital, unable to pop up and pee. Each unfree task of the day requires help. Someone has to open the shades. Someone has to get me a bedpan, close the curtain around my bed, crank the metal bar of the hospital bed down. Fetch the pan when I'm done.

Someone has to bring me that kidney-shaped aluminum pan and a cup of water to brush my teeth. Someone has to take it away. Each task takes too long, every move is slowed down.

Two orderlies carry me to the solarium. The sun's moving. Suddenly the city's buildings are lit by the rising sun. Building after building lines up in shadow, in light. A place of worship, the world is washed from this height.

꧁꧂

Sixteen now, I love to drive fast. I'm back at school, as if I had never left. I take my parents' two-toned Olds after a fight. I'm furious, on fire. Don't know why, don't care either. I speed to the water, park, go sit on the rocks.

I love to drive to the Long Island Sound and watch the water. The other day I made a painting of the rocks. I looked down at my paint tubes, got a coffee can, and mixed water with blues. I put my hand in the can of blue water, then spritzed and splashed the canvas, splattered the rocks over and over, opening and closing my fist. Art is great. It's a great way to move.

⚹

FDR is driving fast through the Georgia backwoods. He loves to drive too. He designed his car with gizmos so he can locomote himself. He's driving a dirt road to Dowdell's Knob, up Pine Crest. It's the high rock outcropping where he spends hours gazing at the changing light on the woods below.

Sometimes he wears his braces outside his pants so he can get them off by himself up there, a great pleasure.

For him, any kind of locomotion will do. FDR loves boating too, so he buys himself an old beat-up houseboat. And he is the first president in history to fly in an airplane. He is reportedly so excited when he takes off that he acts like a sixteen-year-old. He writes:

> We flew north along the Coast . . . . Then inland over the desert. . . . Not flat at all & not as light as I had thought—more a brown yellow with lots of rocks and wind erosion. . . .
>
> Then ahead a great chain of mountains—snowy top . . . .
>
> I tried a few whiffs of oxygen . . . .
>
> North of the Mts. we suddenly descended over the first oasis of Marrakech . . . . We may go there if Casablanca is bombed.
>
> At last . . . . Casablanca & the ocean came in sight.

14

There FDR had secret war meetings with Churchill, whose daughter tells what happened a few days later:

> [My father and the President] set off together for a brief holiday across the Moroccan desert to Marrakech. My father said to the President, "You cannot come all of this way and not see the sun set over the Atlas Mountains from Marrakech."
>
> At the golden hour, the President had to be carried up to the tower. He was determined to see it from where my father said it should be seen. They sat at the top of the tower and they watched the sun set over the Atlas Mountains.

What a sight it must have been—the desert, the sun slipping behind the mountains, the president of the United States of America being carried up to such a height.

Franklin Roosevelt was often cheerful after he got polio, insistent that he would conquer his disease. He hated pity. But soon after he was carried up the mountains in Morocco to see the sun set, he blurted out to his pal Louis Howe, "Why has God forsaken me?"

History is confusing. It is like a braid—you and I and everyone else interweave. History is big, history is small. History happened to you and to everyone too. History is hard to grasp, no matter how hard you try.

Did you know that during World War II, Roosevelt would secretly return to his home in Hyde Park, where he had a recurring dream. There he'd be, speeding down the hills on his sled in the deep snow.

Ship Ahoy

FDR's Houseboat Years

While I was writing about my childhood polio, in crept President Franklin Delano Roosevelt. When I got sick, the thought of him provided comfort like a grandfather, a blood relative who had always been around. Both my parents had worked on his presidential campaigns. The name Roosevelt was part of the sound of our household.

As I was writing my polio stories, I had my parents' set of FDR's private letters, four fat navy-blue tomes edited by his son Elliott, on the floor near my desk. When writing about my illness became too intense to proceed, I would pick up one of the volumes and browse. My illness had been something I never thought or talked about. Reading the private words of this historical figure calmed me down so I could move forward.

Just before I tackled writing about my polio, I had spent a couple of years writing a fictional tale about two gay lovers who lived in sixteenth-century India, a subject far removed from my life. I believe that traveling so far afield in my mind was preparation for writing what was closest to me.

One day leafing through FDR's letters, I got lucky. I stumbled on Roosevelt's nautical log in which he reported on his personal life during the years he owned his houseboat, the *Larooco*. His words were captivating. I was bolstered by the fact that he, like me, loved the water, both born under the sign of the water-bearer, Aquarius. Our shared passion for fishing made him feel even closer.

I wanted other readers to fall under the spell of the personal side of this beloved historical figure. So, after completing my polio book, I embarked on writing about a small slice of FDR's private life.

I was intent on setting down the historical record of FDR's time on his boat as accurately as possible. Imagination would have no place here. Spending days at the FDR archives in Hyde Park, New York with the concrete shreds from his life helped: his grocery lists, personal letters, crooked faded photographs, notes. What follows is as close as I could get to the facts.

⁂

During the roaring twenties, a politically ambitious young man who had been crippled by polio bought a houseboat so he could cruise the warm waters of the Florida Keys and try to cure his damaged legs. When Franklin Delano Roosevelt was stricken with the disease in 1921, he withdrew from public life. He spent three winters aboard his houseboat, from 1924 to 1926. While on the boat, he kept a log in longhand in a three-ring binder, writing in it almost every day. Sometimes he used black ink, sometimes turquoise, pages full of playfulness.

> Grog in midst of glorious sunset
> which was almost as poetic in coloring
> as Frances' and Missy's nighties

So he documented one jolly evening. Or reporting on a broken motor:

> Miami Engine doctor at work
> Patient may respond to heroic treatment

18

Roosevelt had always loved boats and water. When he was five, in his first letter to his mother, he enclosed his drawing of sailboats.

One night in August 1921, thirty-four years after he mailed that letter—after he boated, after he fought a forest fire and swam with his children in the Bay of Fundy—he was struck by polio. Roosevelt never walked again.

On August 28, the *New York Times* found it newsworthy to report his illness, though not its exact nature and seriousness.

FRANKLIN D. ROOSEVELT BETTER

Franklin D. Roosevelt, former Assistant Secretary of the United States Navy, who had been seriously ill at his Summer home at Campobello, N.B. is recovering slowly. He caught a heavy cold and was threatened with pneumonia. Mrs. Roosevelt and their children are with him.

From then on, FDR tried treatment after treatment in his quest to walk again. Two years later, filled with hopes of healing, he rented a houseboat called the *Weona* and spent a month and a half in the Florida waters, fishing, relaxing, and entertaining guests. From the boat, he wrote his mother, Sara, "This warmth and exercise is doing lots of good," and said his visiting guests "are great fun to have on board in this somewhat negligee existence. All wander around in pyjamas, nighties and bathing suits!"

For FDR's health, his wife, Eleanor, felt compelled to visit the boat, but she disliked the blithe atmosphere. "I tried fishing but had no skill and no luck, when we anchored at night and the wind blew, it all seemed eerie and menacing to me." She left the *Weona* after a few days.

In the summer of 1923, Roosevelt traveled from his home in New York to vacation with Louis Howe, his close political adviser, at Howe's cottage on Horseneck Beach in Massachusetts. Missy LeHand, FDR's assistant, stayed there too, taking care of correspondence. At the beach, Roosevelt tried out new regimens for his legs, working with a well-known neurologist, Dr. William McDonald, who had developed a strenuous course of treatment. FDR jokingly said that if he ever became president, the doctor would be the first visitor to the White House. Many mornings Howe brought him breakfast and said, "This is to make you strong. I will see that you become President of the United States."

Sometimes Roosevelt went to the dunes in an old bathing suit, found a secluded spot, and crawled on his hands and knees over the hot sand until he was worn out. Back at the cottage, Howe would fix drinks for the two of them. Picture FDR sipping a martini and discussing politics, having just crawled across the beach. He didn't mind crawling because he could do that himself. What he hated was for others to have to carry him from place to place.

One day that summer, his old college friend John Lawrence stopped by the Howe cottage for a visit. He and his wife had been guests on the *Weona* the winter before. There at Horseneck Beach, the men hatched a plan to buy a houseboat of their own for the coming winter months.

FDR began the search. "What I am looking for is a boat that is fairly low in the water so that I can easily drop overboard and crawl back on deck." In the fall, he found "a real bargain" on Long Island in New York. He wrote to Lawrence, "The owner is apparently up against it financially, and must sell quick!"

The two bought the houseboat, named *Roamer*, for $3,750. Her length overall was 71 feet. She was 19 feet in the beam and drew 3.6 feet. Her hull was about 15 years old and was planked with cypress. She had two 35-horsepower engines.

About renaming the boat, FDR wrote to Lawrence, "It has been suggested that we call her the 'Larose' or the 'Rosela', both of which are euphonious and illustrate the new partnership of Lawrence, Roosevelt and Co." Lawrence replied, "How would you like LAROOCO (Lawrence Roosevelt Co.). The double O and seven letters have usually been typical of good luck in yachts." And so the *Roamer* became the *Larooco*.

As the men prepared for their time on the boat, FDR sent Lawrence a list of who should contribute what.

<pre>
                MEMORANDUM
        J.S.L.   &   F.D.R.

 1. To be attended to by J.S.L.

        Purchase & have shipped to F.D.R.,
        49 E. 65th St., N.Y. so as to arrive
        prior to November 8th:

        Cotton sheets - 48 single for cabin ($2 each)
                        15   "   " crew ($1.50 ")

        Pillow cases to cover 20" x 28" pillows -
                        36 for cabin (50¢ each)
                        15 for crew (36¢   ")

        Towels - 108 face towels @ 20¢
                  48 bath   "   @ 50¢
                  50 yards dish toweling.

        Cretonne - 1 roll for curtains & sofa pillows

        Eastern Yacht club private signal - absent
        pennant & any old yacht ensign.
        (ABOVE PRICES ARE MACY'S)
</pre>

```
2.  To be attended to by F.D.R.

        Silver ware - nickel plated knives, forks
                      & spoons - steel knives carving
                      set -

        Blankets - 12 pair army blankets.

        Bed Pillows - 12 for cabin
                       5 for crew
                      12 sofa pillows

        Crockery  - complete for cabin
        Glassware -     "      "     "

        Beds - 2 white enamel 7' x 3'
                1 bed solid construction 7' x 2½'

        Mattress - 2 for 7' x 2½' bed
```

Missy LeHand, becoming more and more indispensable, was the hostess on the *Larooco*. She had become FDR's private secretary the year before he got polio. A capable, tall, dark-haired, blue-eyed twenty-two-year-old, she was game for fun. At the head of the crew were Robert and Dora Morris, an older married couple from Connecticut, who were paid $125 per month. Captain Morris sailed the boat, and Mrs. Morris cooked and did the housekeeping. The young mechanic George Dyer tried his best to keep the feeble engines running, as did Myles McNichols, known as Mac. LeRoy Jones, FDR's Black valet, woke him each morning, bathed him, and dressed him.

Roosevelt had the boat sailed from Long Island to the Florida Keys. From the start, it was unreliable. He reported to Lawrence:

Dear John:

The LAROOCO has last been heard from at Bordentown, N.J.,— i.e., where the Raritan Canal comes out into the Delaware, engines apparently working all right, but the steering cable to the rudder broke twice and Captain Morris had to get a brand new cable as the old one was rotting out. . . . (SHE IS LEAKING!)

For three winters, FDR lived on the *Larooco*, fishing and swimming and sunbathing, entertaining friends, drinking, and playing games, but most of all tending to his body so that he might walk again. About heading south to find a cure, he explained to one of his doctors:

> You doctors have sure got imaginations! Have any of your people thought of distilling the remains of King Tut-ankh-amen? The serum might put new life into some of our mutual friends. In the meantime, I am going to Florida to let nature take its course— nothing like Old Mother Nature, anyway!

Roosevelt had been assistant secretary of the navy under Woodrow Wilson and had run unsuccessfully for vice-president in 1920. In 1921, before he got sick, he became vice-president of the New York office of the Fidelity and Deposit Company of Maryland, an insurance firm. Post-polio, in the fall of 1924, FDR and Basil O'Connor, a lawyer who had given him legal advice in the early 1920s, opened a law practice in New York City. Although FDR was active—he knew no other way—these years were the most politically withdrawn time of his life. When approached to reenter politics, he vowed that when he could walk without crutches, he would.

During this period, the Roosevelts' marriage was shifting. When FDR contracted polio, Eleanor ignored their estrangement, which had come about three years earlier when she learned of her husband's affair with her social secretary, Lucy Mercer. At that time, she offered him a divorce, which he refused, promising not to see Mercer again, but from then on, they never slept in the same bed. When he got sick, she chose to nurse him with undivided devotion, tending to all his most basic needs.

Both Franklin and Eleanor were driven and passionate. As he withdrew to Florida in hopes of healing himself with warmth and water, she overcame her shyness and turned herself into a public figure, ostensibly to keep the Roosevelt name alive.

The year after FDR bought the houseboat, he helped build a separate home for Eleanor and two of her friends, a couple she met when the three worked for the Women's Division of the New York State Democratic Committee. Nancy Cook was a curly-haired, irreverent, dynamic woman in her thirties, and Marion Dickerman, seven years her junior, was an educator.

One summer day, Franklin and the three women were picnicking by the Fall Kill Creek, two miles from the main Roosevelt house in Hyde Park, New York. The women began to worry aloud that FDR's mother would be closing the house up for the winter and they wouldn't have a place to visit until the following spring.

> "But aren't you girls silly?" said Franklin, "This isn't mother's land. I bought this acreage myself. . . . Why shouldn't you three have a cottage here of your own, so you could come and go as you please?"

So began the building project of the "honeymoon cottage," as FDR called it, which he supervised hands-on. He wrote to his daughter, Anna, on July 20, 1925:

> I have been awfully busy with Mr. Clinton getting prices on lumber, stone work, plumbing, etc. and yesterday telegraphed a bid to Mother and Nan and Marion on behalf of Clinton and Roosevelt, which, if they take, will save them over $4,000! Your Pa is some little contractor!

Both husband and wife created cozy, casual, independent living arrangements for themselves. As Eleanor was settling in to the new cottage with Nancy and Marion, FDR was taking up winter residency on the *Larooco* with Missy. Interestingly, Eleanor was close to Missy; she bought her clothes and treated her like a core family member. And FDR was close to Nancy and Marion; he inscribed an old children's book for Marion, *Little Marion's Pilgrimage:*

> For My Little Pilgrim, whose Progress is always Upward and Onward, to the Things of Beauty and the Thoughts of Love, and of Light, from her affectionate Uncle Franklin. On the occasion of the opening of the Love Nest on the Val-Kill.
>
> January 1, 1926.

Although Franklin and Eleanor spent little time together, they remained in constant communication, always aware of each other's doings. While FDR was trying to come to terms both physically and psychologically with his being crippled, Eleanor was carving out an independent private and public course in navigating the world. They found a way to be apart and together that appeared to suit them both. One can only guess how large the toll of hurt.

Missy reported, in spite of the general jolly mood on the boat, "It was noon before he could pull himself out of depression and greet his guests wearing his lighthearted façade." Eleanor made a few short visits to the houseboat and found it distasteful. Many friends came and went, as did two of the older Roosevelt children, James and Elliott.

After FDR's first winter on the houseboat, he was introduced to Warm Springs, a Georgia spa town. After the third winter, he was ready to say goodbye to the boat and plunge into the Warm Springs waters, which he felt were more likely to heal his legs: "The water put me where I am, and the water has to put me back," he said. Here his focus widened as he founded a rehabilitation center, working to heal not only his own stricken body but others paralyzed by polio.

⟪⟫

On September 18, 1926, when a historic hurricane hit Florida, hundreds of people died and thousands were injured. Damage to property was enormous, and the *Larooco* was nearly destroyed.

FDR had planned to sell the houseboat anyway because his attention had turned to Warm Springs. As he once said, talking about the fun of sailing, "If you're headed for somewhere and the wind changes, you just change your mind and go somewhere else." One month after he disembarked from the *Larooco* for the last time, he bought the former Victorian spa resort at Warm Springs, where he established a therapeutic haven for polio patients. The *New York Times* took note.

F.D. ROOSEVELT BUYS SPA
Acquires Warm Springs, (Ga.) Property
from G.F. Peabody of New York

WARM SPRINGS, GA., April 26 (AP).
Announcement was made today of the purchase of the Warm Springs resort by Franklin D. Roosevelt of New York, former Assistant Secretary of the Navy, from George Foster Peabody, also of New York. The purchase price was not given.

The Warm Springs property consists of several thousand acres of land, a hotel and several cottages and swimming pools, together with the springs, which flow at the rate of 1,800 gallons per minute. Mr. Roosevelt said he expected to make the property an all-year resort.

Doc Roosevelt, as he came to be called, was filled with sympathy for others with polio. Soon his sympathy extended to all those less fortunate than he was. In later years, Louis Howe looked back on FDR's evolution in the aftermath of polio.

> You see, he had a thousand interests. You couldn't pin him down. He rode, he swam, he played golf, he sailed, he collected stamps, he politicked, he did about every damn thing under the sun a man could think of doing. Then suddenly there he was flat on his back, with nothing to do but think. He began to read, he began to think, he talked, he gathered people around him—his thoughts expanded, his horizon widened. He began to see the other fellow's point of view. He thought of others who were ill and affected and in want. He dwelt on things which had not bothered him much before. Lying there, he grew bigger day by day.

As FDR's focus was expanding at Warm Springs, Eleanor's focus at Val-Kill was expanding too. She and her cohorts built a larger building next to Stone Cottage for their new business, Val-Kill Industries. They taught local farm workers new skills so they could manufacture early American furniture, pewter pieces, and weavings to help supplement their dwindling incomes.

FDR continued his intimate relationships with several women. Whether they were sexual or not is a matter of dispute among historians, but according to one medical report, he displayed no symptoms of *impotentia coeundi* (sexual dysfunction). Missy was always at his side until she had a stroke in 1941. She had been opposed to the sale of the *Larooco*, and soon after the last cruise she suffered a nervous breakdown and was hospitalized. But she returned to work a few months later and continued her role as hostess in Warm Springs.

In 1926, when FDR published *Whither Bound?*, a lecture to prep school students at the Milton Academy to mark the establishment of an Alumni War Memorial Foundation, he wrote to Lucy Mercer, "I dedicate this little work, my first, to you." When FDR died nineteen years later, Lucy was with him.

At the same time, Eleanor was becoming a significant public figure independent of Franklin. Privately, she blossomed too, delighting in the company of Nancy, Marion, and others in their crowd. A few years later, she became a close companion of her handsome bodyguard Earl Miller, a New York State trooper and former welterweight champion. He taught her how to ride and bought her a horse. He took her target shooting and taught her to use a pistol. Earl became an intimate member of the extended family, eating meals with them, as did Missy.

⋘⋙

Soon after the first *Larooco* cruise, FDR promised himself that he wouldn't reenter politics until he could walk without crutches, but he broke that vow in late 1924 when he delivered the presidential nominating speech for Governor Al Smith. His teenage son James walked him to the podium. James later recalled the occasion.

> I was afraid and I know he was too. As we walked—struggled, really—down the aisle to the rear of the platform, he leaned heavily on my arm, gripping me so hard it hurt.
>
> Leaning forward, he rested one crutch against (the rostrum) and raised one arm to wave at the crowd. He was still smiling. The crowd gave him an ovation.
>
> He never again was as popular, as he was in that instant. It has been dramatized, but no re-enactment could capture the intensity of the drama that was played out that day.

FDR was the star shining that night, although Smith lost the nomination. Four years later, Roosevelt fully reentered the fray and was elected governor of New York. The stock market crashed one year later. The roaring twenties were over. The Great Depression began. In the midst of it all, in 1932, Franklin Delano Roosevelt, still unable to walk, was elected president of the United States.

Two:

Pleasures

Jamali Kamali
Airborne in History

This is a story about how history and imagination infect one another unwittingly. It's also a story about how my door to mystical happenings, previously slammed shut, opened a bit. It starts with a man named Jamali. Jamali was a sixteenth-century Sufi court poet who lived in Delhi, India. According to Delhi's oral tradition, he had a male lover named Kamali, although no one knows for sure who Kamali was. For nearly five hundred years, this unwritten story has traveled down through the generations.

I stumbled upon these characters while I was at the Sanskriti Foundation in Delhi for a month-long writing residency. One week after I arrived, the residents were told that later that day, we would have a chance to visit the newly restored Jamali Kamali Mosque and Tomb. It was about to open to the public. O. P. Jain, the founder of Sanskriti, was a major supporter of the restoration, thus this outing. The conservator of the restoration would guide us at the site.

Our bus arrived at an overgrown park entrance where we traipsed alongside a river full of plastic garbage, climbed through hills of brush, stumbled over unrestored ruins, and finally arrived on top of a hill, a plateau, where the Jamali Kamali Mosque and Tomb stood. At its entrance, a brand-new sign informed visitors that the tomb held the remains of Jamali, a sixteenth-century Sufi court poet and saint, and a person named Kamali, whose identity was unknown.

When we entered the small space of the tomb, I was stunned by its beauty. Two white marble graves sat side by side on the floor. The red and blue circular ceiling was decorated with sunbursts and floral forms carved in plaster. A band of Jamali's verses encircled the ceiling. The conservator spoke, "Some have thought Kamali was Jamali's wife or perhaps his brother. Others have thought that Kamali was a disciple of Jamali, the saint. The undisputable fact is that both were men. A symbolic pen box, traditionally a sign of a male, is carved on each of their tombs. It is believed, through our oral tradition in Delhi, that Kamali was Jamali's homosexual lover."

"But" I said, "the new sign out there that you just put up says his identity was unknown."

The conservator explained that in India a public sign would never mention homosexuality.

Jarred and inspired by that fractured moment as well as the intimate beauty of the tomb, I returned to my Delhi desk, and, to my surprise, I began to write as if I were Jamali speaking to Kamali. The imaginary sound of their voices propelled me forward. I had neither plan nor goal. Seeing the beauty of their graves, hearing the tale that had been passed down, spurred me on to invent a story of love, sex, separation, and death. It is not based on any historical record—there isn't one. But for the next three weeks, every day I sat at my Delhi desk and wrote.

The night before I was flying home to Massachusetts, the Sanskriti administrator knocked at my door and said that O. P. Jain had heard about my poem. He was coming to Sanskriti in a little while and wanted to hear what I had written. So that evening, I read my pages aloud to O. P. and a small group of artists. One man said he thought that I was inhabited by Jamali, channeling him. His comments rolled right off me. I thought he was misguided but kept that to myself.

While at Sanskriti, I hounded the people in the office with questions like "Did apples grow in Delhi in the 1500s?" Although the poem was a fiction, the physical details had to be accurate. Finally, they put me in touch with Bruce Wannell, a Persian scholar from York, England, who answered question after question as the poem unfolded.

A few facts are known about Jamali—where he traveled, the Mughal emperors he befriended, and that he was killed in battle in Gujarat—and are included in the poem. For the next year and a half, I kept writing.

I wrote one section during a month in Nova Scotia on Cape Sable Island, living in a trailer overlooking the ocean as the fog came and went. Mostly, I wrote at home. It didn't matter where I was. Whatever was in front of me, leaves blowing or a bird hopping, appeared in the poem. I was comfortably living in the world of the characters. A year and a half passed and finally, Jamali and Kamali had had their say. The book was done.

Many people have asked, "Why did YOU write this book?" I'm not a man. I'm not gay. I'm not Indian. I'm not Muslim. I'm not a Mughal scholar. I'm not an art historian. I'm a straight, white, American, Jewish, 21st-century woman. And I'm not even young! I've crossed so many lines here—gender, sexual orientation, time, hemisphere, etc. So often, writers are advised to "write what you know." I did the opposite. Call it imagination.

Opening oneself to the unknown paves the way for a large exploration rather than the up-close, confining details of "what I know." The unknown is a wider plain—a big, flat, open space where options abound. The endless screen makes possible a roomier grasp of universals, like love, death, separation. It makes possible "what is known by all" rather than the smallness of "what I know." There is largesse.

⸙

When *Jamali-Kamali* came out in the United States, friends and relatives gathered in my hometown bookstore to celebrate. In attendance was my old therapist. Afterwards he came up to me and said, "The flags are unfurled! This book is your whole unconscious!" Did the story spring unfettered and fresh from my imagination? Was I inadvertently mining my personal history to imagine this love story? Was I channeling the spirits of Jamali and Kamali so they could tell their story, as many have believed? Was I unknowingly braiding together Jamali and Kamali's history and my own? Was the story somewhat true, somewhat factual? Curiously, a few people have asked me if my poem is a translation of an ancient text.

I do not believe that Jamali and Kamali took over my body and spoke through my poem. To explain this in earthly terms i.e., "The spirits of the two men chose me to tell their story," is too of-this-world, too bricks and mortar. But something was going on. The truth is elusive.

Writing these two men into life was unlike any writing experience I had before. Certainly, while working on a poem, I have felt inspiration, but never sustained for so long. It felt "given."

Supernatural means "attributed to some force beyond scientific understanding or the laws of nature." Before writing *Jamali-Kamali*, the kind of things that happen to everyone happened to me. For example, for a few years after I graduated high school, every few months I would think about a particular friend, then the next day he would call. Not dramatic, but noticeable. I thought it was an odd coincidence.

36

A striking recent example. One of the loves of my life died a short time ago. I visited a mutual friend to find comfort.

As I was leaving, she said, "Did you use honeysuckle shampoo to wash your hair?"

No, I said.

"Are you wearing honeysuckle perfume?"

"No."

She was so curious about the smell, she looked up its meaning and later emailed me this: "Honeysuckle represents the flames of love, and the tenderness for love that has been lost." Not attempting a logical explanation, I do believe that something unexplainable was going on.

Here's a different kind of example. Now when I see a butterfly, I often say "Hi Mom." All to say, since writing *Jamali-Kamali*, an aspect of my lived experience has shifted and enlarged in a roundabout way. Although I don't believe that the spirits of the two men chose me to tell their story, I do think that opening the passageways for whatever might come clears the air for unexplainable forces to breathe. It is beyond consciousness. Perhaps that's what "given" means.

The Jamali Kamali Mosque and Tomb is said to be inhabited by djinns and ghosts. In the Koran, djinns are earthbound spirits that appear as animals or humans. Numerous people have reported all kinds of sightings over the years. Laughing voices, animals growling, apparitions—the list goes on. I was unaware of this when I visited the site. Maybe the notion that the site is haunted plays a role in the question of channeling.

I went back to India in 2011 to celebrate the publication of *Jamali-Kamali: A Tale of Passion in Mughal India,* bringing the book to the Jaipur Literary Festival. Bipin Shah, of Mapin Publishing, arranged the Delhi launch beforehand. As I read from the book, Jamali's and Kamali's voices filled the room. Afterwards the moderator, a well-known cultural figure, opened a discussion by attacking me. I was shocked and surprised that he had been chosen to moderate the evening and suspect that Mr. Shah was as well.

"You distort history by fictionalizing it!" he said.

Then I talked about the place and power of the imagination. The eloquent audience broke out into intense but polite arguing, making for a thought-provoking evening.

To me, at that point, it was clear that fact and fiction were two separatable entities. I wasn't "distorting history," I was inspired by a snippet of history to make up my own story and saw no conflict. It's not as if my fiction would alter the historical record.

That's what I thought until, a few years ago, I looked up my *Jamali-Kamali* book title on the web to see how it was faring and found myself on a travel portal to Delhi. I was reading about the historical monument, the Jamali Kamali Mosque and Tomb—which subway to take for your visit, opens at sunrise, closes at sunset, Thai restaurant nearby—when I landed on something unexpected:

Jamali Kamali offers a fine piece of structural design and a fascinating story behind it.

Forlorn Love

After his death in 1535, Jamali was buried in his tomb alongside Kamali. Very few are aware that both these men were deeply in love with each other. In Jamali's poetic works you can find passionate words and phrases describing his immense love for Kamali such as "On the map of your body, there is nowhere I would not travel."

The "fascinating story" behind the monument is a fiction. It comes from my imagined poem, not from historical facts. Jamali did not write the line quoted above. I did. The webpage relates a few details about Jamali's life as if they are facts, but the details are taken from my invented poem. The website recommends my book, *Jamali-Kamali: A Tale of Passion in Mughal India*, to learn more about the men's histories. I immediately emailed the people at the website and asked them to correct their mistake, which they did. Relieved to have set things straight, I thought that was that.

But now, eleven years after my book was published, an article came out in CitySpidey, a media company in New Delhi, "How the tomb of Jamali-Kamali enabled the Queer Community to claim their spaces." An excerpt:

> Many stories are told about the tomb of Jamali-Kamali. Some believe both of them to be brothers. At the same time, another story is that of Kamali being the wife of Jamali. However, the tomb's structure represents a man being buried. However, the Indian queer community sees this tomb as a ray of hope for queer history, which had been ignored.
>
> Karen Chase's work on the tomb further tries to legitimate this claim. Chase writes that the verses inscribed are of love. In *Jamali-Kamali: A Tale of Passion in Mughal India*, Chase cites the verse:
>
> > In the plump dusk, I hear a peacock screech
> > eye marks on my lover's neck Kamali, let's go to the
> > lake to moisten our love scars.
> > I will wash mud from your muscled legs.
> > My secrets rest in the wedding hut.
> > I visit another man as the moon circles down.
> > Come my protégé, my Kamali to bed. I will show
> > you moves of a new planet as no astrologer could.

Again, my imagined story has found its way into what is called history. The verses cited above are from my poem. They are not the verses written by Jamali that encircle the ceiling of the tomb. Bruce Wannell, the Mughal scholar whom I consulted on research matters, visited the Jamali Kamali tomb and translated Jamali's ceiling verses from Persian. These are included at the end of *Jamali-Kamali*. Writing the story of Jamali Kamali was not "work to legitimize" anything.

And again, yesterday, while working on this essay, I looked up my Jamali Kamali book on the web and found a new example of my poem polluting history, cited as fact. I will not send corrections. History is not a factual record. Rather it is a messy conglomeration of fact, fiction, and truth. It is beyond my control, like it or not.

I cannot help but wonder if the stories told in these pages connect. One story is how this writer followed her art wherever it led, to imagine a tale plucked from who knows where. The other story is how her tale is becoming woven into Indian history. Maybe my Jamali Kamali story is true and surfaced for enigmatic reasons. Maybe it is a "historical" text about homosexual men in India. There is no way to know.

But I do know this: as Salman Rushdie said, "Sometimes legends make reality, and become more useful than the facts." And Jamali and Kamali, thanks to the impure way history forms itself, move deeper into the Indian story—history coming alive through art.

Hedgeballs and Rinkydinks

A mother and son singing "America the Beautiful" as the road gets eaten up and day's light turns to pitch dark. Dots of headlights dart to the raspy low jazz notes. Neon signs flash in reds and greens and oranges, the speedometer lit up, and our first day has passed. We are getting close to Morgantown, West Virginia, the stopping point for the first night. It has been 500 miles and 12 hours.

Last fall, my younger son Matthew flew to my home in Lenox, Massachusetts from his home in Santa Fe. A few days later, we set out for New Mexico—mother and son, together in a car from prelight dawn to postlight dark for five days straight, autumn on the trees and sunshine on the land. To start, I drove.

"You excited?" Matthew asked.

"Yes!"

"Okay amber waves of grain, here we come!" he said.

Wanting to get out of the familiar East, we mostly drove interstates that first day. After pizza for lunch in a northern New Jersey town, we crossed into Pennsylvania on I-80. Matthew remembered that Frank Lloyd Wright's house, Fallingwater, was in the state, so we found a Visitor's Center and called to make a reservation, only to learn that we were so far away we could never make it before closing time.

We knew where we were starting, we knew where we were ending, we knew how long we had, and the rest was spur of the moment. Where to stop, what road to take, where to eat, where to pull over, when to make time, what to listen to, when to talk, when to be quiet—unfolding like breathing, planless life at its best.

Driving west through Pennsylvania, we're singing "Morning Morgantown" along with Joni Mitchell's high-pitched voice from the moon. We sing and shuffle with the music across the country.

"Let's each have our own room when we stop," I suggested.

"Of course," Matthew blurted out, "after we've spent the whole day together, we'll need time apart."

"I'll treat you."

"No, I'll treat you. You're doing me a favor to help get the old car out to Santa Fe."

We agreed to alternate.

Late that afternoon, as we were heading south on a small road, the sun just low in the sky, we drove up and down Amish hills, passing horse-drawn tractors, large-hatted men, road signs depicting a horse and buggy and saying, "Share the Road." The light on the steep hills was heartbreaking—not the wild, shaking light one sees at the ocean, but a timeless, orangey Old Masters light, varnished and composed.

Because I was in my early twenties when I gave birth to my sons, we grew up together. In those years, I was mistaken for their older sister or the babysitter. The last trip I made with Matthew was when I was the age he is now, forty-four, and he was living in Paris with Julie, who would become his wife. I was giving a paper at the University of Barcelona, where he joined me. Then we took an overnight train under a navy star-studded sky along the shore of the Mediterranean back to Paris, where he had an exhibit of his sculptures at a small museum. All memorable.

Day 2 was morning in Morgantown, guided by our early morning singing. In the lifting dark, at the Ramada Inn, we nibbled on an oversized buffet breakfast. In the car, as Matthew pored over the maps, I rearranged the boxes in the back seat. It was full of things from my father's house: a microscope, rubber boots, Tiffany candlesticks, an axe, and cartons of books. My father, the ninety-one-year-old grandfather Matthew had been close to, had recently died.

We decided to head south toward Kentucky. I took the wheel, and we pulled out of the hotel parking lot. The first day we had crossed the Hudson and the Susquehanna, and as we left town, we crossed the Monongahela. Soon we were driving up and down winding West Virginia roads, forested and unmapped. Without accompaniment, and with overdone soppiness, we belted out "West Virginia, mountain mama, country roads, take me home."

We were in the middle of nowhere. When we saw a stopped pickup truck, we pulled over. "Excuse me, sir, does this road go to Smithfield?" Matthew asked.

Long pause as the guy sized up dark-haired, dark-eyed Matthew.

"Well, you *can* get there that way."

We kept driving.

Matthew turned on the music. On came a voice chanting Hare Krishna, a white westerner named Krishna Das. Matthew began to chant too, and then, first hesitating, I joined in. Our chanting wove on through the snaking hills.

Son and mother chanting loud and long, passing through those woods, a word bubbles up to consciousness. Holding one note, chatting between *Hares*, going in and out of the notes, switching styles of chanting—it was *holy*.

Why so much chanting? Last summer, just months after my father died, my first husband, the father of my sons, had suddenly fallen ill. Together, Matthew and his older brother, David, and their families flew to California, where they nursed their father through his last alive week.

At a pause in the chanting, I told Matthew a story of a blind date I dodged when I was in college. A friend of mine was dating Timothy Leary, who had a friend named Richard Alpert. Both professors at Harvard, they were experimenting with LSD and magic mushrooms. One weekend I was due to travel to Cambridge for a date with Alpert, but I backed out, scared by the thought of hallucinogens. Richard Alpert later became known as Baba Ram Dass. Soon afterwards, I met Matthew's father at a civil rights conference. He showed me some peyote buttons his roommate had given him, along with the warning that they made you vomit. He tossed them out of his Saab into a nearby garbage pail, we talked about freedom rides, and we began to get to know each other. Two years later, we were married.

When Matthew was eleven and David was thirteen, Dick Chase precipitously walked out the door, after having been an especially loving father. Following years of ups and downs between father and sons, in recent times there had been meaningful mending.

We crossed a bridge: "Welcome to Ohio." Driving along the Ohio River still chanting, we came upon a power plant and stopped the car. Smokestacks, coal barges, sculptural concrete buildings, ethereal billows of carbon spewing into the sky—hideousness and beauty, both. We filmed, we photographed, we talked about coal and carbon. One lone man walked back and forth over a long barge.

Matthew took a lot of videos at the power plant—clips of red and yellow leaves floating down the Ohio, with smoke reflected in the water.

"Beauty and the beast," he mumbled as we walked back to the car.

That second morning we stopped in New Martinsville, West Virginia, for a second breakfast at Presto Lunch. Eating my pancakes,

I thought of "Autumn Begins in Martin's Ferry, Ohio," a poem by James Wright. His line "All the proud fathers are ashamed to go home" popped into my head. Did geography suggest the poem, or was I thinking about the father of my sons? The waitress told me that Martin's Ferry was up the river not far from there, but in the opposite direction from where we were headed.

In the afternoon, we took the ring road around Cincinnati, then onto an interstate heading toward Louisville. Truck headlights came on.

"Louaville, y'all," Matthew said.

"Lou a ville," I responded. Playing with our accents, we tossed the word back and forth.

In his southern drawl, Matthew recalled asking for directions earlier that day. "The guy said, 'Ya go over the bridge, and ya turn at the place they call Rinkydinks.'"

"He was a guy," I said, "with this round ole hat on and a big beard coming down all covered with hair, red shirt, ya know he was in a truck, honey."

"Then we passed the place they call Rinkydinks and the sign that said Dinks. It's called Dinks but everyone calls it Rinkydinks, but its real name, its Christian name, is Dinks," added Matthew. We could not stop laughing.

Just north of Louisville, we found a Super 8 Motel in La Grange, Kentucky, in a mall behind a Cracker Barrel. We found a Mexican restaurant with raucous sounds and long lines coming out the door. It was Elvis impersonation night. We left and found another Mexican restaurant, crowded and lousy, then off to the motel.

We said goodnight and went into our rooms. I began to think about home. Each night I would call my husband once I got to my room, moving from one anchor to another. In fact when I told my husband this on the phone, he said, "It's funny that you feel that."

"Funny? What do you mean, funny?"

"Oedipal," my psychologist husband said.

"I think Oedipus is in the back seat of the car on this trip," I joked.

⁂

Maps of Indiana, Illinois, and Missouri, our day 3 states, show straight roads. Driving into the Midwest, we stopped to explore a rusty, red field of dry soybeans, then drove on a road the same color. We drove through the town of Cynthiana, Indiana, then past it.

Somewhere in Illinois we pulled up to a cornfield and parked. There was an oil well that looked like a hammer going up and down in the middle of the field. I had never seen or smelled one.

"Ew," I exclaimed, "smells like money."

We walked over and through dry corn stalks, yellow kernels on the ground, scattered reddish cobs. The heavy red and black steel machine was stunning—a rhythmic clink clink clink, the sound of oil being sucked up from the earth and machine parts moving up, down, and around. I stood there hypnotized as Matthew, a photographer and sculptor, focused on filming the rig for a long while.

Back on the road, we passed enormous fields of corn, sorghum, and soybeans, nary a family farm. Then we passed a grain elevator, the lone dominating structure of the towns in these parts. With Matthew at the wheel, I mentioned that he had done most of the driving.

He said, "Like right now I'm passing someone but I can't totally see over that hill and you would be really nervous. Sometimes you hit the brake a little bit, being cautious, and I don't use the brake much. I might take my foot off the gas. So it's a little jerky, which is fine, I can handle it! It's not like you're just cruisin' on for ten hours at a time, no sweat. I think it takes more of your *chi* than it takes of mine."

"What's *chi*?"

"*Chi* is like your life force, your energy, your calories. Whoops! What!" He caught himself veering toward the shoulder. Much laughter.

Finally, St. Louis came into view. Then we saw the Saarinen Arch, which first appeared small. As we got closer, we saw how huge it is, then saw the bridge over the thrilling, muddy Mississippi. At that point, the stainless-steel-covered arch, the Gateway to the West, took my breath away. It's the tallest monument in the country at 630 magnificent feet.

Matthew pointed out how simple the structure is—it's a parabolic arch—and held up a string to show me what that meant. "Think of the *M* of McDonald's. It's two parabolic arches."

From the time my sons were little, both of them were sponges for knowledge. This they inherited from their father. Soon after I met their dad, we were driving over the Third Avenue Bridge into New York City. While he was driving, with a piece of paper on the dashboard, he was drawing a diagram to show how different strains of philosophy developed—fascinating and scary.

My father, a scientist at heart, was in love with knowledge as well. The last conversation I had with him before he began his long slide away occurred the day he finished my new book of poetry. He loved the book, but also had analyzed the thought processes behind the poems.

He said, "We think differently. There is a lot I can learn from the way you think."

I realized that the men in my life have been intent keepers of knowledge, bolstering my tendency, as well as allowing me the freedom, to think far and wide.

After the Arch, we got in the car and explored St. Louis: boarded-up neighborhoods, marble and brick downtown architecture, the Anheuser-Busch section that reeked of hops. We had trouble finding our way out of the city but finally came upon an interstate. Then came the silliest hours of the trip: scat singing to whatever music came on, then a rendition of "Ruby Tuesday," sung a capella by Matthew, filmed for his niece, Ruby. When we stopped for gas, we both got out of the car, still infected with silliness. A puzzled-looking female customer started to stare at us, as if thinking, "Who is this giggling twosome? Who are these funny foreigners?"

So I spoke up. "Hi. We're driving my old car out to my son's house in New Mexico. He's taking it over. I'm from Massachusetts. He's my son," nodding toward Matthew.

Gratefully, she answered, "I noticed your tags. I was wondering."

A little while later, we pulled onto a hilly back road, heading toward Kansas. It was still light, and we were clipping along at a good pace. As it got dark, our headlights shimmered and glowed off the yellow divider line. It felt very far out there, like we were coming into the land's center.

Once we got to Nevada, Missouri, we found a motel. I liked that our rooms were connected by an inside door. "Goodnight, Maff," I said, and closed the door.

***

The next morning, we wake up in our adjoining motel rooms in the dark. We have a routine that combines getting an early start with allowing us each to get enough sleep. Whoever wakes up first emails the other "I'm up." When the other person awakes, he or she checks his or her laptop, receives the email, then knocks at the other person's door. Both early risers, we always get going before dawn breaks.

We each grab a donut and cup of coffee as we leave the yellow-lit, slightly shabby motel lobby and drive a few miles to the Kansas border. The sun begins to rise on Route 54 as we come into Fort Scott. The music shuffles to "Farm Girl" and we mumble to Ry Cooder's steady, laid-back song. The streetlights are lit but about to be shut off. One pickup on the road, but otherwise folks have not yet ventured out. We pass through the town slowly, then drive a straight road lined by fields. On comes Dylan's "One More Cup of Coffee." Am I imagining that it echoes some old Hebrew melody? Our voices lower, then trail off. The land starts to flatten.

I am remembering when I was living in Cambridge, in the sixties. One gorgeous day, I was walking over to Brattle Street. Roundly pregnant with my first son, David, and newly a Harvard student, I was newly engaged in domestic pleasures. Feeling swell and beautiful, I walked into Design Research, itself a swell and beautiful housewares store. A sound I had never heard before was ringing through the place, Bob Dylan on the record player. There and then, I fell in love.

"One more cup of coffee for the road," Dylan's voice is filling the car. We see a tree with unfamiliar fruit on the side of the road, so we bring the car to a stop. By now, the sky is plain primary blue, the tree's skinny branches are gray, the few leaves left are lime green. Some fruit hang from the tree, many are on the ground. They are the color of the yellowest corn, the size of a grapefruit, and the texture of a brain. We crush one, put another in the car.

"These are some strange fruit," Matthew mumbles.

Now we are in Gas, Kansas, sorry we don't need gas. Now we are in Iola, and I think of the poem "Iola, Kansas," by my long gone pal Amy Clampitt. "I feel my heart go out, out here in the middle of nowhere."

Matthew exclaims, "We found it!" when we reach Eureka. Archimedes is with us. We sing less as the road unfolds.

As we keep driving this long straight road, we notice Krause Farm Equipment and swerve into their parking lot. We drive round and around, filming the red and yellow, black and green steel beasts, this zoo full of machines that work these vast farms: Arctic Cat, Agco, Gleaner, New Idea, White, Kubota, Woods.

I am absorbing a new geography, the core of the map. In the

past, the corners of the country have intrigued me and I have visited three: Key West, Florida; Neah Bay, Washington; and Lubec, Maine. The fourth, Imperial Beach, California, near where my first husband lived, is the missing corner. But now, Kansas, the heart of the country, lands me on a crossroads of feeling as we steer further into the interior.

When Dick Chase left, the sordid details of our divorce and the turmoil it caused crowded out the possibility of much contact. We were estranged for years, and he was on the outer edge of my life. Now, with his sudden actual death, I, to my surprise, was drawn to mourn the richness he had brought to our family's young years.

We get off Route 54 onto the most rural roads of the trip, many of them dirt. Because they form a grid, we figure we can't get lost. Then we realize we are.

As a truck approaches, I say, "Why don't you stop the car, I'll get out and flag the truck down to find out where we are."

"What would be the fun of that?" Matthew says and keeps driving.

It's fine with me since I trust we'll find our way out sooner or later. We pass long-horned cattle, sorghum fields, soybean fields, lone farmhouses, and then come to a huge number of hay bales in a field.

We stop.

Matthew gets out and gathers his camera equipment.

I say, "Take as long as you want, I'm going for a walk."

He jumps a fence, runs far and fast toward the bales. His large frame slowly becomes a tiny dot in the distance.

The sight reminds me of a scene I watched over and over when I was a little girl. My father liked to swim across a nearby lake. A towering figure, he would dive into the water, then begin his powerful crawl. By the time he reached the other shore, he too was a tiny dot in the distance.

I meander up the road and see a large snakeskin hanging on

a fence. The wind picks up, the high blowing grass looks oceanic. We are at the lower end of the Flint Hills.

As I walk past the snakeskin, another picture comes to mind from a long-ago trip to the ocean. I was pregnant. The wind was wild and the sky dark gray. Suddenly the sun came out, the wind stopped, and I went for a walk on the beach. I took my sneakers off. At that moment, I felt movement in my belly. It was David, my firstborn! My feet in the wet sand, the shining water, and the hot sun bonded me to this earth. Why so many images of water, why so many thoughts of mothers and sons, of fathers and daughters?

Matthew and I meet back at the car and take off. We keep spotting hawks. Matthew points out that because they normally perch in high places and nothing's high here, they have to perch low, making them visible. We stop again when we see a large dead owl, remove two feathers. Eventually we come to a paved road to discover we have driven way out of the way. Soon, on our right, a large lake appears. The wind is still wild and we stop again. Waves on the water make it look like an inland ocean. We walk out onto a skinny jetty. Matthew is filming the wind pushing everything around. My red shirt is blowing all over the place as is my hair, and the waves are breaking behind me. I am kneeling over, examining rocks.

"I think these are fossils. Do you remember when you were little we visited the Mudds and hiked to a creek that had tons of fossils? These look just like them."

Matthew says, "Yeah, wasn't that in Oneonta? Didn't Lucia's mother make some yummy lemon cake when we got there?"

His boyhood memory builds on my young mother memory and becomes the current story. The huge wind has transformed the scene into something surrealistic and timeless.

He could be six. I think of one day when our family was at our cabin in the Adirondack Mountains. He was mucking around, down at the pond with his father. I was inside, listening to a Joe

51

Cocker record. Matthew looked up at me in the picture window and I looked out at him. I began to sway my arms to the smooth crusty voice singing "You Are So Beautiful to Me." Matthew began to sway his arms in unison.

Finally we walk back to the car. Matthew mentions that when he gets home, boxes of items from his father's house will have arrived. He studies the Kansas map to figure out a route. While rearranging the stuff in the back seat, I am struck by the ordinary things Matthew chose to take from my father's house: his axe, his boots, a saw, a jacket—things my father held in his hands and wore on his body. I notice the books he chose from my father's shelves: Dickens, Stein, Miller, Mowat, a twenty-volume set of *The Book of Knowledge*, the ancient edition my father nearly memorized as a child.

I took collections of letters: van Gogh's, Freud's, Pound's. But the book I read first was *Farthest North*, by the Norwegian explorer Fridtjof Nansen, who explored the Arctic in the 1890s with his boat *Fram* and his crew. Two maps were included with the book. As I was reading, these maps were stretched out on a table so I could precisely follow Nansen's account of courage, discovery, and hardship. I took breaks from reading and worked on poems about my father's demise and death.

Matthew folds up the Kansas map, and we head slightly north of Wichita, then travel west on 50.

"You are such a good navigator and such a good driver. I'm not exactly sure what I bring to the mix on this trip."

"Enthusiasm," he replies.

We stop in some small town, and I take the strange fruit from the back seat into a secondhand store. I ask the saleswoman if she knows what it is.

"A hedgeball," she exclaims. She tells us that they are not edible, but that if you set them under a porch or in a basement, they repel scorpions and other insects.

Back in the car, we both kid around with the word *hedgeball*, stretching it out, stressing each syllable, indulging our shared love of sound.

We stop in a town with extremely wide red-brick streets. We stop in a town that looks decidedly western, which makes me wonder where does the West begin? In the town where we pick up Route 50, we find a hip grocery store where we buy good cheese, good bread, and, sadly, rancid corn chips. We pass through Hutchinson, where one of my favorite poets, Bill Stafford, was born. "Who are you really, wanderer?" he wrote. We pass through Stafford, no relation to Bill. We come to Spearville, where we pass a field of huge windmill parts, then fields and fields of windmills, then Garden City, then Dodge City, which we speed through like the prairie wind.

The land has become absolutely flat. Neither of us speaks much. Eventually, feedlots begin to appear. Thousands of cows jammed together, unable to move, the sight and stink atrocious. These are mammals? We start to talk about cows. We start to talk about happiness, about beef, about chickens. Our conversation turns fragmented.

I point out a farmhouse far off the road, set in a field with nothing around, grass blowing hard against the treeless, huge sky.

"Would you want to live in a place like that, out in the middle of nowhere?" I ask.

"God, no, I'd want a hill, a canyon. Gimme anything."

"I would. I really would. It feels open like the ocean."

We come to a sign for Holcomb.

I say, "Holcomb, hmm. I think that's the town where the *In Cold Blood* murders happened. I just changed my mind about that farmhouse." We know how to make each other laugh, and laugh we do.

As light wanes and we are getting closer to the Colorado border, the sky turns purple, red, pink, and orange. Matthew croons along with The Band: "And when you get to the end, you wanna start all over again."

Stark black silhouettes of trees line the road's shoulders against that canvas of a huge red-splayed sky. Black lines of huge steel irrigators are winging across the fields in the near dark. Matthew is driving. The sight of his profile and his hands on the wheel are stirring. Approaching the border, we pass through the blackest night.

Earth, air, fire, water—Kansas contains the elements: fire in the night sky, wild water at the lake, windy air blowing like mad, and the dirt in field after field. Kansas, the Ur state.

We cross into Colorado and land in Lamar. Matthew goes to the office of a nice looking motel to inquire about availability.

"They have two rooms, but they are not next to each other. One's upstairs and one's downstairs."

Forget that—I want to be close. Let's go somewhere else."

Down the street, we check in to the Cow Palace.

⟪⟫

Each day, the changing light had framed time's turning. Our last day was the first one we would not see dark turn to light, then light turn to night. We wanted to reach Santa Fe by afternoon. This five-day romance was about to end.

In the oncoming morning light, we left Lamar. It was flat as flattest Kansas. Then, suddenly, far away and small, the Rockies appeared on the horizon. The outside world began to surface. Matthew got a text message from an old friend in Colorado who had been following our Facebook posts and realized we might be able to get together in Alamosa. Our timing was off, so we didn't meet up with him. Then we stopped in a store where I bought a hat for a friend's newborn. Then each of our cell phones rang. The cocoon of the car started to undo.

We arrived at the enormous mountains, then drove through a pass. We detoured north to Great Sand Dunes National Park, the highest dunes in North America. I was videotaping our approach to the dunes when Matthew started to tell me about the scene at his father's house a few days before he died, how they got marijuana for him. Matthew was describing private personal scenes.

"No one needs this to be recorded," I said, and turned off the camcorder. We hiked the dunes in the blazing sun.

When Dick became ill, not only did his sons and their families hurry to his side, but many other family members arrived. After Dick left our family, he had numerous marriages, relationships, and other children. He and I had little contact. But in recent years, we spoke occasionally, and at length. Even so, my tangled feelings kept me away.

Instead, my focus was on my sons' loss. I spoke with each of them on the phone every day. Adult separation collapsed for a while. It was only after we returned to a relaxed rhythm of contact that I began to realize my own sadness at Dick's death. We each had lost our fathers this year—really Matthew had lost two. We each were ready for some good times.

Since Matthew has been an adult, he and his family have lived across the country. In spite of that, we've remained close via phone and cross-country visits. Spending extended time together has made it possible to fully relish our shared love of music, words, adventure, travel, and art, as well as undergo our recent losses of each of our fathers. And thanks to a car, some time, and those amber waves of grain, was it ever a pleasure for this son and this mother.

That last day, we drove from Colorado to New Mexico, through Tres Piedras, through Ojo Caliente, through Espanola right down into Santa Fe—that beautiful familiar land—and pulled into Matthew's driveway. The late afternoon light that day was jewel-like. Circe, the family's Australian shepherd, ran out to greet us, followed by my daughter-in-law and grandson.

55

We slowly got out of the car and headed toward the house. Once inside, we sat down at the kitchen table with Julie and Quill and began to relate our tale.

Artist Statements

Lil Block, my mother, was an accomplished abstract painter. She chose never to show her work. Painting was personal, the larger world irrelevant. I grew up in a household where making art was as natural as climbing a tree or setting the table.

Every Saturday when I was four years old, my mother took me to New York City on the train to take art lessons in the basement of the Metropolitan Museum of Art. Looking out the window at the water as the train crossed the Harlem River was thrilling. It meant we were getting close. I can still smell those jars of red, yellow, and blue paint sitting on the oversized wooden easels. I have been making art since then.

Both of my Russian-Jewish immigrant grandmothers were art makers. One worked in the garment district as a seamstress, and painted canvas after canvas of semirealistic scenes of New York City. The other sewed intricate costumes for dolls which would get auctioned off for charities. Making art has run in our familial blood for generations.

Constructed Space

It must have been about 1947—not long after the war—in Interlaken Gardens, a garden apartment complex in Tuckahoe, a suburb of New York City. I lived there with my parents, Zenas and Lil Block, and my brother, Richard. Ed and Evelyn Zern, my parents' best friends, lived there too, with Brook and Erica. The two families were back and forth between the apartments.

A bedroom in the Zerns' apartment had two doors, the door to the bedroom and the closet door. If you opened them both the right amount, they formed a small triangle of space with the wall of the room. Brook and I would construct that space, then go in and laugh and talk. He must have been four or five, so I must have been three or four. Being with Brook in that created triangle was magical.

Hanging in a hallway outside that room was a large piece of newsprint paper with rows of different colored dots crayoned across the page. Brook had made it. What exuberance—the colors, the rows, the dots! My first memory of seeing art. I've not stopped looking since.

As an older child, I was struck by my mother's crayoned abstract/cubist drawing in our downstairs entranceway. Later I was stunned by Pollock's *Blue Poles* at MoMA, dizzied by the sheer size of it, the drips, the splatters, the active, alive use of paint. My heart nearly stopped when I saw the marble-carved body of Michelangelo's *David* in Florence. Pure beauty. How could I not mention the Rothko Chapel in Houston seen on a work trip twenty years ago? Helen Frankenthaler last year! Two days ago, meeting with my art group, six painters who gather monthly. The list is endless. Looking at art is as constant in my daily life as anything.

Looking at art is one thing. Doing it is another.

Body of Work

This canvas was my thick gouache period,
this, from my primary color period,
this one, my experiment with grids.

Today, in my basement, painting,
I boomerang back from one wet canvas to another,
one packed with glittery spirit,
the other moves like fury.

Each one arrives
from this arm, this hand,
this leg, brain or feet.
They thrust, get talky,
go silent, scream.
These, my body of work period.

In high school, I spent two summers at the Art Students League in New York City, and, for the first time, painted with acrylics, which were perfect for me. I loved that they were water soluble and dried fast. Water was all-important.

One day at the Art Students League, I was making a painting of the water at a seaside park near where I lived, a scene I loved to paint. I found a tin can on a shelf, mixed blue paint with water, put my hand in the can, and kept flinging the watery mixture at the canvas. After all, I was born under the sign of the water-bearer. Charles Alston, the teacher, came over.

"What are you doing?"

"I'm the water," I said.

Luckily, he said, "Alchemy!" and with a big smile walked away. I was getting physical via the blue water, leaving behind my self as art led the way, took its own course.

During college, I made a painting of Hemingway in thick blues and whites, a closeup of his very alive face. It was the summer he killed himself. Not long after, I was a young mother with two baby sons and had a tiny studio in our New York City apartment. There, I made mirror collages. I would load my sons into the stroller and walk down Columbus Avenue to collect free scraps of mirrors from a glass store. Once home, I would pound them into pieces, then glue the chips and slabs onto wood, making unusual reflections. While my sons were growing up, I spent time spinning, dyeing, and weaving as well as painting.

Twelve years ago, I made a studio in my basement and began painting in earnest and ever since have been switching back and forth between painting and writing. Right now, I am dyeing raw canvas and collaging that onto painted canvas in a series called The Erie Canal. I love canvas.

Ode to Canvas

He found him in a desert land, and in the waste howling wilderness; he led him about, he instructed him, he kept him as the apple of his eye.

—Deuteronomy 32:10

Things happen to you, canvas.
You have paint brushed on your flat surface.
You have paint splattered on it.
You have charcoal drawn across your middle.

I hose you down,
I embrace you, then attack you.
I turn you yellow.
I turn you white,
I turn you blue.

You are the apple of my eye.
I turn you to the wall.
It's time to hide.

Canvas, you surprise me.
Your spirit balloons up and down,
you turn paint to mud
or drip a red stream.

Whatever happens to you,
I reflect upon.
I follow your lead, enhance.
On and off, I take over.

I am your pupil and you are mine.
We reflect each other in the round, dark center of our eyes.
I try to see what you are up to.

I turn you clockwise.
I turn you counterclockwise.
I turn you upside down.
Canvas, I am in awe of you.

Let's go play.
Let's go heave the world around.
You got your job, I've got mine.

My Working Style

I start with a large canvas on the floor and walk around it and begin. Nothing in mind—I don't want anything in mind. I start putting paint on the canvas. Then more paint. I get rid of things. I add things. I add a lot of things. I get rid of a lot of things.

When something starts to look representational, I get rid of it—it's confining. Seeing a literal anything, like a tree or a face or a mountain, suggests a path. Pathless freedom is what I seek, the mental wordless muck of color, line, and form.

In the later stages of a painting, I hoist the canvas onto my easel. I stop moving. I sit still and muse, consider what I am seeing. I make small changes. Often it takes me a few months to be satisfied that a painting is finished.

Into the Stars

On the morning of February 1, 2017, I called Jonathan Matson, my literary agent. After many rings, Laurie, his wife, picked up the phone. She told me that Jonathan had died of a heart attack the day before. In shock—we both cried. A vibrant, life-loving 67-year-old man was suddenly gone.

I spent the next six weeks in my basement studio, absorbed, submerged. When my grief was starting to subside, I made a series of Jonathan paintings. The five abstract paintings look like the curvy, star-splattered sky in shades of black, white, a muted yellow, gray, bits of gold. He had disappeared into the stars.

I wanted to share the paintings with Laurie, his widow, whom I did not know. So I took photographs of each painting and glued them into an album which I sent to her. She wrote me a gracious reply.

Fast forward five years to last December when I received a Christmas letter from Laurie for the first time, the widely-sent kind of letter that summarizes family news. I'm reading along about Jonathan's new grandchild and this and that and I come to a paragraph that begins: "Karen Chase, a client of Jon's, painted a series of amazing abstract paintings in the weeks after Jon died . . ." I was surprised, then overwhelmed.

I wrote to Laurie, offering her the paintings, as well as giving her an out because they are large and they are abstract, not to most people's liking. A quick response—yes, she would love to have them. She is adding a new room to her house and the paintings will have their own wall in that room.

Two weeks ago, my husband and I drove the three hours to her house on the north shore of Boston and delivered the paintings to the house Jonathan and Laurie had lived in since they were newly married forty years earlier. There, the paintings will hang.

Painting *Into the Stars* allowed me to change my grief into something new, to make grief and love concrete. Painting *Into the Stars* gave me the chance to offer Jonathan's wife a gift.

The Iceland Effect

So why did I become a writer? In my late twenties, my husband and I took our two young sons to Iceland for two weeks. The barren landscape was shocking.

With extra gas cans strapped to the roof of a rented Land Rover, we headed for Askja, a live volcano in the interior of Iceland. There we stayed in a cabin built for Neil Armstrong while he was training for the first human voyage to the moon. NASA had chosen the site because it was the place on earth that most resembled the moon. The sight stripped me bare.

After Iceland, writing became primary, and art took second place. Before Iceland, I had not written much at all. But after seeing that stark landscape, I was beset with writing poems. Something woke up inside me that necessitated verbalization. I was shocked into using words in new ways. Seeing such extreme barrenness evoked thoughts and emotions that made saying words out loud, meaning talking, not expressive enough. The written word offered something beyond speech. I didn't make a decision, a choice, to start writing. It happened to me. This must be why most writers write.

My Writing and My Painting

Painting is sensual—the paint, the brushes, the canvas, the water—while writing requires thought and articulation. Abstract painting rejects verbalization. But if painting is representational, by definition, words are part of the equation. Take van Gogh's *Starry Night*. Aside from the power of the painting, words come to you as you look at it—tree, sky, hills, town, church. However, when you look at a Rothko, it is beyond words. Conscious or not, you register wordless form, wordless color, wordless composition. The impact of an abstract painting is nonverbal or even preverbal.

For me, painting is physical. Listening to music, I move around my studio. I am carting my canvas outside, I am turning it upside down, then this way, then that way. I am hosing it down with water. I am shaking it for the paint to drip and scatter the right way. My painting are characterized by motion—the result, I believe, of my childhood polio.

For me, writing also involves movement, but it is mental movement. My brain travels hither and yon, tries to discover, invents, tries to make contact with my reader. When I was a girl with polio, laid up in bed, this was the kind of movement I could do. Now I sit here at my desk and compose. When I write, I am still in the silence, my brain hard at work. Maybe because of my lifelong art-making, I find painting to be mostly playful, as opposed to the always challenging written word.

A Poet's Job on the Ward

Teaching poetry writing to troubled teenage girls at a school in rural Massachusetts came to an abrupt end. Two very large, rough female employees each took me by an arm, escorted me to my car, stood there while I got in, slammed the car door, and bid me adieu.

"No poet's ever gonna set foot on this campus again. Get the hell outta here."

I had been working at Valleyview for a year, and the inhumanness toward the girls had come to an ugly abusive head. I had alerted Children's Protective Services and, of course, was immediately banished.

Teaching writing in an earlier setting had sparked the evolution of this work. While teaching in Connecticut's Poets-in-the-Schools program, I had noticed that many students who had trouble in school liked to write poems. Teenage boys who caused chaos in the classroom and made fun of "the poetry lady" were curious when I would show them a pail of garbage and talk about how poems can be about anything—eggshells, one old shoe, last week's newspaper. Eventually, some of them turned seriously to writing. Perhaps these students were drawn to poetry because it contains a strong thread of rebellion, an aspect of poems I emphasized.

Later, when I began to work at Valleyview, the girls explained that they hated poetry because it had "big words" and was about "serious things like love." When I handed them onions and asked them to write a love poem to an onion, one girl said, "What do you want me to write? 'I love you, onion. You make me cry. You're so dirty. Your skin is so wrinkled.' Anyway, how can you love something dirty?"

You can write things in poems that don't seem to make sense, I told them.

Another girl suddenly said, "I love it. You can turn a toad into a train!" She had schizophrenia. When she talked to herself, she talked only about her illness. When she wrote, the world rather than her sickness became her subject. Her odd use of language was intriguing.

"Write all the time—between chores, before dinner," I told her. "Make what you've written say exactly what you want it to say."

When I left Valleyview, I had a year's additional grant money from a foundation to continue teaching poetry writing, but no place to do it. The grant was based on the view that almost everyone gets satisfaction from expressing themselves in a creative way, whether they wish for it or not, so give people that chance. With grant in hand, I visited an array of jails and hospitals in or near New York City, armed with the belief that poetry belongs in places it doesn't belong. Gun-shy from my school job, I searched for a humane setting to teach poetry writing, one where I would receive excellent supervision.

When I visited New York Hospital-Cornell Medical Center in White Plains, it seemed like a fine place to explore my early ideas and questions. Here was a high-quality psychiatric teaching hospital with a wide array of people with varying points of view. And I was not unfamiliar with hospitals. As a child with polio, I had been in and out of them, so I knew, apart from everything else, how isolating illness could be.

NYH-CMC's psychiatric residency program made for a lively academic climate in which it was possible for me to learn about psychological illness. The wards offered opportunities for research and training, reflecting diverse views. Some stressed a pharmacological approach to mental illness; others emphasized psychotherapy or behavioral programs. One approach did not exclude the others; rather it was a question of emphasis.

The people accepted for treatment there had been hospitalized repeatedly and had shown they couldn't exist in the outside world. Most of what they did was explored as an expression of pathology. When a poet teaches writing on the ward, there is an opportunity for something else. The poet can read the patient's poem as a potential work of art that is effective or not, rather than as another expression of pathology. I was lucky to find a staff who shared my view.

In time, as the Hospital Poet, I was conducting weekly poetry workshops and individual writing meetings with patients, conferring with clinicians, receiving supervision, offering writing workshops for the staff, and fully participating in case conferences. Eventually we—I say *we* because by then I was wholeheartedly a member of the staff—noticed significant changes in some of the patients. I began to work closely with a few clinicians to try to better understand what might be happening. The project grew. Workers from unrelated fields, poetry and medicine, embarked on a thoughtful collaboration. Fortunately, this was a time when wide-ranging exploration was still possible in psychiatric teaching hospitals.

※

People take turns talking. One speaks, then the other. If each person listens, hears, and responds to what the other has said, their speech is collaborative. When a silent man named Ben and I met, we took turns writing, and in time our writing became more collaborative. In some ways, our written collaborations mirrored what happens when people speak, but a major difference was that we assumed we could remain silent. I made no push for us to talk.

People who have been through traumas sometimes stop speaking. After he was put away in St. Elizabeth's Hospital, Ezra Pound became silent. After the man who raped her was murdered, so did Maya Angelou. After Elie Wiesel survived Auschwitz, he took a vow of silence for ten years. What draws a silent person back into the world of words? How does a silent, or silenced, person bear witness to what has caused them to shut up?

People have countless ways to express themselves. Whether a person's life has been traumatic because of external events or because of inner turmoil, or whether a person's life has been relatively free of troubles, many of us eventually want to bear witness to our individual experience. People sing songs to bear witness, they reveal themselves over beers in bars, they tell their stories in support groups, they paint paintings to bear witness. What makes someone listen with attention to himself, claim his life as something worthy of disclosure?

The first nearly silent patient I wrote with once told me, "Ten years ago, I was half asleep all the time. The only thing that went in and the only thing that came out was poetry. My verbal skills were excellent, but I couldn't deal with people. The only contact I had was through writing." Making contact with another person can entice someone to come forward and bear witness individually, and so can making art.

Artists work in isolation and they work together with other artists. Jazz relies on collaboration; players have to listen hard and spontaneously respond when they improvise. But most artists work individually on their creations, either in solitude or within a community. They work in their houses, in coffee shops, in studios, wherever they can be alone. Being part of a community also nourishes creative work. In the last century, the salons of

Bloomsbury and cafes of Paris provided a place for artists to meet. Today, writers' conferences spring up all over the map for writers to affirm their citizenry. Poetry slams are everywhere. Poetry communities form in big cities and out-of-the-way towns where a great, rich range of people come together to read and perform their poems, as well as register their like or dislike of what they hear.

In some cultures, poets ordinarily compose poems together. In small villages in Morocco, for example, poets can go on for hours, as anthropologist Clifford Geertz notes: "Poets sing alternately, sometimes the whole night long, as the crowd shouts its judgment, until one retires, bested by the other."

When I first came to the hospital, I mainly ran poetry workshops with small groups of patients. To begin, I would suggest that we all write a poem together, since that was a way people could be less afraid to write and share the burden of the page. People could also maintain a sense of distance by writing a group poem. Once I xeroxed Wallace Stevens' poem "Thirteen Ways of Looking at a Blackbird" and handed it out to the people in the workshop. Each person read a stanza aloud in his or her own style—some slow, some fast, some staccato, some smooth. Since there were words people didn't know, one fellow looked them up in the dictionary and chimed in definitions as we continued reading. Someone asked what *inflection* meant. To illustrate, I made inflections with my voice. A patient began to make blackbird inflections with hers. I said that the poem regards blackbirds from different perspectives, that we were regarding the poem from different perspectives and voicing them with our own particular sounds. The room took on the sound of a low concert, each of us different instruments in the orchestra. Afterwards, we wrote a group poem about birds.

Eventually, some of the students' desire to express themselves outweighed their desire for the comfort, fun, and stimulation of collaboration, so they wrote on their own.

Ray, a sad and articulate young man who had been active in the workshop for many months, became completely silent. He stopped eating and had to be fed intravenously. One day, after ten months of silence, I told him that the workshop was about to meet and that we would be listening to Scott Joplin piano rags before writing. With no words, he refused to join us.

Moments later, Ray walked into the room and began to mime playing the piano. I replied by doing the same. We were going to write a poem, I said, I would write a word, then he could say a word which I would write down. After I wrote *piano,* it was his turn. He sighed and appeared caught in the knowledge that saying the word *no* was saying a word, something he did not yet want to do. When I wrote "(sigh)," he laughed. Then he added a few words.

He rejoined the workshop and wrote poems with other patients, with me, and on his own. Simultaneously, he started to speak again. Although it is impossible to know why, he was brought back into the community of words, in part while writing collaborative poems.

Many questions about collaboration arose when I wrote with patients. The first always was would the person meet with me or not? Most often, I chose to work with someone who was hesitant to speak. But I also taught patients who used words too easily as if they did not weigh much. Patients may have met with me for a number of reasons. They may have liked me because I seemed like a regular person. Or they may have liked me because I seemed like an odd person. Or they thought poets have some glory or specialness that might rub off, or they were writers or wanted to be writers, so they thought I might be able to teach them something. They may have felt pushed into it or they didn't really want to meet with me but they were scared to refuse. Of course, not all patients agreed to meet with me. They may have refused because I seemed scary or in the past writing had seemed too powerful and frightening. Or they thought they were too disabled to write. Maybe they valued poetry and felt that working on it in a mental hospital was a violation. Or they were afraid of the pressure of work, or that meeting would be a waste of their time or my time.

With some patients, writing poems together seemed all wrong, not something to aspire to. And with some, writing collaboratively happened in roundabout ways. Beth, a highly educated woman in her thirties, came to the ward after she had been found psychotic and naked in the center of Stockholm. She spoke in a formal style that kept the staff and patients at bay. She walked around with a clipboard in hand and jotted down notes. Although Beth participated in the life of the ward, speaking freely at meetings and activities, her comments were extremely superficial. During our first meeting, she quizzed me about my thoughts on formal aspects of poetry, using words like *anapest, metonymy, hexameter*. At one point, I suggested that she try to be *careless* and *thoughtless* when she wrote in our meetings. She studiously jotted down my suggestion on her clipboard. Already, we were alerting each other about aspects of our own linguistic styles.

I gave her some scraps of wallpaper from an old house, suggesting that she write a list of words that the wallpaper evoked.

When I asked her to choose the five most powerful words from the list, she said, "Should I choose them for their meaning?"

That question was her first show of unconventionality, because the conventional interpretation of my suggestion would have been to choose the words for their meaning. Instructed by her question, I asked her to choose them for their sound. I read the words out loud, repeating them so she could take in their sound. When she wrote, her words had hints of expressiveness.

In later meetings, I sometimes gave her Rilke's poems in

71

German, a language she did not know, and asked her to write her own poems based on the sound of Rilke's lines. Eventually, she wrote in her own dense, stark, evocative style. Words seemed to take on a new force for Beth. They seemed to be a tool rather than a barrier.

With some patients, finding a language to write together preceded finding their own style. With Beth, it happened the other way around. Nine months passed before we started writing collaborative poems. Each was a production, in which we would add a few stanzas every week, editing as we went along. The common style we evolved was softer than her own—careful, precise, and very visual.

How do two people negotiate the ground rules of writing together? Who will initiate the poem? How will the poem be structured? Will each person add one line at a time, one word, or as much as they like? Does each person have the liberty to change the other's words?

When two people write together, how do they agree on a subject? In the early years, I relied on many types of stimuli, objects like stones or onions, tapes of music or animal sounds. The idea was to offer *the third thing* on which the writers could concentrate. Finding a subject sometimes came from what had been written the week before. Or I might ask a patient to choose a line from last week's poem to get started. Sometimes the patient arrived with a subject already in mind.

An array of acrobatics takes place as the work of writing collaborative poems gradually progresses. Who takes the lead in a poem? How does a poem get grounded? Who lets it fly? The boat gets rocked, risks get taken that upset the balance. Who pushes the language boundaries in one way or another?

With great hesitation, silent Ben chose to raise his voice. As we alternated writing lines of poems for two years, our dialogue was the place where Ben's voice gradually became more resounding. We wrote our lines one to the other, never knowing where they would lead. I wrote a line, Ben wrote a line. Ben wrote a line, I wrote a line. Eventually, he began to speak out loud and returned to the talking world.

On the ward, the aim of my job was to give an accurate voice to the self through writing, to help patients choose whether they wanted to use the sound their self makes. It was always the patients' choice.

Even when I worked with severely ill patients, I always turned our work back to the writing. I might say, "Considering how awful you feel these days, how do you think we can move ahead on your writing during these rough times?" In other words, "The work of poetry writing goes on, simultaneous with your troubles. Keep this side of yourself alive, in the midst of misery."

Although a talent for writing is unusual, a need for self-expression is nearly universal. The subject for poems is everywhere—they can be about anything. Whatever triggers a strong personal reaction is a potential subject. None is too small, too ordinary, too bizarre, or too daring. Whatever the subject, poetry requires genuineness. By genuine, I mean personally accurate. The poet tells her personal truth her own way through the poem's form and sound. If she is blessed with talent and is willing to work hard, the reader may see something startling that could not be communicated otherwise. Poems renew words so they ring out fresh from common usage. A poem can show a reader as well as the writer a small part of the world in a new way. The writer can be as surprised as Ben was by his own voice.

With Ben, it was only after he began to write with some expansiveness that the subject of poetry came up. By then each written or spoken word seemed less hard-won, thus less fragile.

On the other hand, when a patient dashed off lots of lines, with no intention of working on the writing, I try to be clear about the place of warm-up exercises, what makes poetry poetry, and how the work of writing may transform an early draft into a poem. For people who use words in a facile way, as if they were weightless, I stressed their weight.

One reason I call what Ben and I wrote *poems* was their high degree of authenticity. His genuineness helped his writing and helped me trust our work together. He seemed to stand behind every word he wrote or said, sparse though they were. Neither pretense nor sentimentality puffed his words. They all seemed heartfelt and there were no false notes. Genuineness took a long time to show with some patients, and with some it never did.

Poets at their most productive are freed by their flexible use of language. Psychiatric patients are often hampered by theirs. The word *play* used by some poets and patients often has different aims. Most poets hope to make contact through this unconventional use of language. But many patients' unusual language isolates them. The most extreme example is when a person makes up their own language, severing contact with others.

The poet in the psychiatric hospital has the job of not just stimulating writing but also teaching how to edit a poem until its qualities move readers to the place the writer wants them to be moved. Poems use language, sound, music, play, form, and meaning. The way these elements are synthesized affects the quality of the poem. When patients used language in an unusual way—punning, rhyming, making up words, condensing them—I tried to point out how this kind of language play could help or hinder the poem.

A poem often combines unrelated images, sometimes called leaps or disjunctures. I tried to teach a kind of revision, how to discard the leaps that obscure the poem and select those that enhance it. The directness with which I talked about this depended entirely on the patient. Ben's relative speechlessness made me generally less direct with him. I highlighted how things can stand for other things in poems.

Sometimes this use of metaphor came too easily, too naturally to patients, as when they made up their own language. Their words stood for things only they could fathom. Inventiveness, usually an asset, worked against them. When one patient wrote, "Louvre tumi sagili tumorlee," he left the rest of the world out. I told him that I had no idea what his line was about.

In the setting of the psychiatric hospital, where patients have many chances to talk about their feelings, I emphasized the process and craft of writing. Certainly, poems must contain feelings, but they must also contain a host of other elements necessary to poetry. For example, when talking about a poem, I may have focused on how its musicality—its rhythm, pauses, stresses—affected the poem's meaning, rather than discussing the poem's meaning per se.

Chronic mental patients lack self-esteem. When a patient has the unusual experience of being regarded as a student, a potential poet, rather than only a sick patient, her self-image may change. The unique experience of writing and working on a poem without exploring its personal meaning can be refreshing and nourishing. Many patients have abilities like humor and originality that are activated when writing poems. These qualities should not lie dormant during illness. When a patient's poem is read by others, the person is no longer a solitary voice, or as one patient said, "a small purple light going on and off in the snow, that no one sees."

Once a patient said to me, "When you write poetry, you get to *use* your mind." His mind had seemed like his enemy because he often imagined he was being followed, mocked, or poisoned. When he wrote poems, he noticed that this same mind could serve him. Writing poems does not cure mental illness. But it can tap into and use the healthy, as well as the ill, parts of a person's mind.

For some people with schizophrenia, words take on the force of things, rather than acting as symbols for things. Hearing the word *fire* might feel the same as fire. Words normally stand midway between the person and the thing, offering the safety of distance. If a person experiences the world with intense immediacy and expresses that vision in a poem, are they reporting, hallucinating, or imagining?

For a teacher on the ward, it is important to keep these distinctions in mind. After writing what seemed like a wonderfully imaginative poem, a patient asked me, "Is it right?" He had wanted to write factually, realistically. And perhaps, for him, this would have been the best, most useful thing.

There are some dangers of being a poet working in a psychiatric hospital. One danger concerns what happens to the patients' poems once they are written. The poems are the patients' property. This is a matter of dignity. They should not be handed over by the poetry teacher to the therapist to be used as takeoff points for therapy. In the same way, I would not suggest to a patient to use a dream told to his therapist as a jumping off point for writing a poem, enticing as that might be. On the other hand, if a patient wants to bring a poem to therapy, that's his business. Or the other way around, if a patient wants to bring a dream to a writing meeting, that's his prerogative. In our writing meeting, I take care to encourage the person to use the dream as a point of departure for a poem, not as a point of departure for psychological exploration. Ben eventually began to initiate talk with his therapist about our meetings, and in a general way, our poems. And throughout, his psychiatrist and I talked in depth about our work with Ben, but the poems themselves were not shared.

Put simply, the psychotherapist has the job of guiding patients toward direct and conscious talk and awareness of their troubles, to help them gain mastery over their inner lives with the goal of greater understanding and the ability to go back out into the world and function. When a patient brings poems to therapy sessions, the psychotherapist has to be on guard not to be diverted or seduced by the poems. This can become a hindrance to their work. Merging therapy and poetry writing dilutes them both, although each is an expressive venture.

Another danger comes when the poet remains distant from the rest of the staff. The work done between patient and poet should not be sacred and separate from other work done on the ward. It is the poems that require protection, not the information about the patient that might surface during the poetry meetings. By information, I mean aspects of a patient that might surface during our meetings but remain hidden elsewhere. If a person speaks gibberish on the ward but is coherent in his poems, this information should be shared. In planning a person's treatment or diagnosing their illness, this kind of information may be critical, and the poet has a responsibility to impart it.

For a worker on the psychiatric ward, it is a challenge to keep sometimes opposed aspects of a patient in mind. A patient may be an imaginative, hardworking writer who otherwise fights with everyone or sleeps. I may see her strengths, and the nurses may see her limitations. We each have to remember the side we don't see, whether we focus on it or not.

Another danger for poets is old as the hills. People tend to romanticize poets. The poet must shun being elevated as a romanticized truth-teller, although being falsely elevated is really being diminished. Sentimentalizing the poet undercuts the potential value for interdisciplinary collaboration between artists and clinicians.

In the movie *Round Midnight*, Dexter Gordon, a real-life saxophonist in the fictional role of Dale Turner, tells how different saxophonists play—how the swing bands play, how Lester Young plays like Debussy, how Charlie Parker plays—all different. "You just don't go out and pick a style off a tree one day. The tree is inside you growing naturally," he says. A poet and a clinician each provide growing conditions for trees, but the conditions are different.

Long ago, Oscar Wilde wrote a sentence that sounds archaic in today's tell-everything culture. "A man is least himself when he speaks as himself. Give him a mask and he will speak the truth." Wilde's words are timeless, because a human's wish for privacy is part of nature, conscious or not. Writing poems offers that mask.

Three:

Horrors

Learning to Shoot

The day of Ray's party, the great rains came. Blue and gray plastic tarps were strewn from tree to pole all across his large yard, and barbecues were stationed all around. From the kitchen speakers, Pink Floyd sang through the late afternoon, and it felt as though the partygoers had boarded one big wet boat harbored in Ray's backyard. Christmas lights were strung from tarp to tarp, and they blinked as it began to get dark.

I sat on a bench talking to my friend Clay, an experienced shooter from a Southern family. Was he packing right then? I asked. To show me, he brushed aside his oversized shirt. There was his pistol, tucked into the waistband of his jeans. Although he often spoke about handguns, I was taken aback. In a moment, what had been just words became real. Then I wondered who else at the party was carrying a gun.

I told Clay about a scare I'd had in the fall. My husband Paul and I had hiked up a Vermont mountain, not passing another soul on the way. On top, as we relaxed in the sun eating our apples and chocolate, a lone man strode up the trail. Tall, thin, and in camouflage gear, he wore a pistol in a holster. He did not look particularly weird, but when we said hi, he said nothing. Instead, he sat on a log fifteen feet away, directly facing us, silently and slowly unlacing his high black boots. If he had wanted to shoot us, there was not a thing in the world we could have done. Had I been armed, would it have been unwise or even crazy to have produced a gun? Probably so. Finally we got up and left.

I then told Clay about another hike, this one in Alaska, that had caused another scare. A few miles into the deep woods, Paul and I saw grizzly bear footprints and fresh scat on a muddy trail. What if we had surprised the bear and what if he had a taste for humans? We would have been at his mercy. As Clay and I talked about self-defense, he offered to take me to the Smith and Wesson shooting range to learn how to shoot. With undue speed, I said no, I didn't have time, I had to work. Learning to shoot seemed out of the question. I am a poet who grew up in the well-heeled, sophisticated Westchester County suburbs of New York City and graduated from Sarah Lawrence College. Shooting is far from these worlds. But I do live in the Berkshire Mountains, and I do have friends and neighbors who farm, hunt, and fish. I have fished the English Channel over torpedoed wrecks. I have even fished at the foot of a live volcano in Alaska, and, seasick, hauled in the biggest halibut on the boat.

I did not sleep much that night as I mulled over Clay's offer. Because I was in the midst of a writing project that touched on men and guns, and because of my few recent hiking scares, I was intrigued. What would it be like to shoot a weapon? I dared myself to say yes to Clay. By morning, I was swayed. I called him.

Clay Max Hall had starred on Broadway as a child and served in army intelligence during the Vietnam War. When he returned from Asia, after a difficult period of readjustment, he enrolled at Harvard and became the head of the Harvard Pistol Club. A man with a long ponytail and an abundantly roving mind, he is one great, complex character.

Before we went to the shooting range, Clay wanted to show me how these machines work. He came over and unpacked his nylon bag of guns onto my kitchen table. He told me his grandfather had lots of guns, unlike his intellectual father. Clay showed me the pistol he carries, a semiautomatic Smith and Wesson .45. He bragged that he can unzip his fly completely without losing the gun. He emptied the bullets from the magazine and let me hold the pistol.

Clay, a natural teacher, wanted to impress upon me the striking differences in the way various guns looked, felt, and mechanically operated. His care and thoroughness made me feel safe. He took out a revolver, then a target practice pistol, then a tiny Beretta pistol. *What a sexy gun*, I thought, small, light, and beautifully designed, a pleasure to hold. *What a jarring thought.* At close range, I could kill someone. There, on the cherrywood table, was an array of dangerous weapons. There, on the counter, was an array of root vegetables for a soup I was going to put up. The clash thrilled me as I broke into a sweat.

I held each handgun. Clay showed me how you don't put your finger on the trigger, except to shoot; how you hold both arms up and straight out; how you line up the sights. I was thankful Clay had brought the guns to my calm kitchen, a cozy place to begin to handle these tools that humans have used for centuries, tools I might learn to use. Clay packed the weapons back into his bag.

I told him about Operation Berkshire, a sting operation of a few decades ago, which was the subject of my writing project. In this part of New England, a group of hunters had been poaching black bears and selling their gallbladders to middlemen, who in turn sold them in Asia for use as aphrodisiacs and intestinal medicine. For two years, two environmental cops posed as rogue hunters and became part of the gang. Then one winter day, twenty-five hunters were simultaneously arrested in four states at six o'clock in the morning.

During my research for this project, I talked to these men on the wrong side of the law and came to feel uncomfortably far from understanding what drove them. If I learned to shoot at a shooting range, I could come closer to their world in a secure way. Learning about guns might help me better grasp the whole story of Operation Berkshire.

Why was I drawn to this story of Operation Berkshire in the first place? As a little girl, I loved fairy tales—the scarier, the better. Wild beasts roamed the mountains and forests on the pages of my Grimms and Andersen volumes. The settings were peopled with villains and heroes. Operation Berkshire contained many of these elements.

Clay and I made a plan to go over to the shooting range. Smith and Wesson offered a course, Massachusetts Carry Permit Course, covering the safety and legalities of firearms use and a few basics of shooting. Upon completion, I would get a certificate, enabling me to march down to my local police station and apply for a Class A unrestricted gun license. Although Clay liked being my guide, a class might be good so I wouldn't take too much of his time.

The next day at Barnes and Noble, I browsed through the periodicals. I picked up *Concealed Carry Handguns*, then put it down as if it were a hot coal. I wanted to buy it but was mortified. I skulked around and then picked up the magazine again. Two teenaged boys with do-rags, metal studs, and tattoos were laughing and looking at magazines nearby. An overweight gray-ponytailed gal was spread out on a bench reading a local women's newspaper. I put the magazine down and left the store.

The next day I set out to make the purchase, but I hadn't checked my purse to see if I had enough cash, and I did not want to use my credit card because there would be a record of the sale with my name on it. For someone relatively free of paranoia, this was new. I walked into the store, headed straight to the magazines, plastered *Concealed Carry Handguns* against my jacket, and approached the cashier. When she asked if I had a Barnes and Noble discount card, I was so jittery that I lied and said yes but I didn't have it with me.

"No problem," she said, and looked up my name on the computer. Of course, she discovered I didn't have a card, and now I really felt like a suspicious character. Was this what folks on the wrong side of the law go through? I didn't have the ten dollars for the magazine, so I put it on my credit card, thinking that if I hesitated, I would seem even more suspicious. Back in my car, I concealed the magazine under the day's mail, and drove off. The words *concealed handguns* seemed nearly as powerful as the actual thing.

The following day, Clay and I set out for Smith and Wesson. We stopped at a diner where a man wore a T-shirt that said:

FREDS SPORTING GOODS
An American Tradition
the only sport
endorsed
by The Founding Fathers

When we arrived at the shooting range, I felt awkward and sober. We suited up for shooting, in what seemed to be slow motion. First Clay handed me a little black container with two oversized bright yellow earplugs that were moldable like erasers. I mushed them around in my fingers, then made one end pointy so it could squish right into my ear. He put his in, I put mine in. Then I took my eyeglasses and put clear plastic shields on the frame piece that goes over the ears. Finally, we put on baseball caps and big blue padded headphones.

We walked down the hall to the shooting range. I held the pistol. I loaded it. I shot the gun. Its kick, its bang, and its odor were intoxicating. I was stunned. Clay advised me not to think about the target. Just get comfortable holding the gun. Always point it downrange. Never have your finger on the trigger until you are going to shoot. The intense effort to focus on nothing but shooting was singularly pleasurable. I signed up for the class on our way out.

Cooking, gardening, sex—I love these elemental activities

that know neither class nor culture. When I shoot, a similar pleasure comes. Shooting is physically and sensually gratifying. The urge to shoot is primitive, arising out of nearly universal fierce and fear-filled feelings, conscious or not. How curious, then, that shooting is scorned in many cultural circles. I wonder and weigh what would be wrong to master shooting, to be extraordinarily cautious and responsible with a gun.

Two weeks passed, and it was the day to drive to my eight-hour class. To quell my rising anxiety, I chose an old Edith Piaf CD for the trip over. *Je ne regrette rien.* Maybe that raspy voice I listened to in my youth gave me courage. I could hear her sound then, the camouflage of a foreign tongue blurring the fact of what I was embarked on. As I drove on the Mass Pike east to Springfield, the morning air was a thick gray pail of mist.

I go in, register, then make my way down the hall to the long, low-ceilinged classroom. Its pinky beige walls are overly lit with fluorescent light. Sixteen students file in and sit at fake wood tables, two to a table. I sit in the front row next to an overweight, well-groomed black woman in her mid-thirties, with a tote bag advertising a bank. She has lots of braids with yellow beads and a great wide smile. Our crew-cutted and mustachioed teacher, Jim, carries a load of keys on his belt. He wears a beige T-shirt with a Smith and Wesson logo, khakis, and suede sneakers. Although he is a policeman in a rough, industrial city, today his job is to teach us about guns, administer a test, then send us on our way with a certificate so we can apply for a gun permit to carry a concealed weapon.

Above the blackboard in front of the room hangs a poster, giving the four cardinal safety rules for firearms:

1. Treat all firearms as if they are loaded.

2. Never permit your muzzle to cover anything which you are unwilling to shoot.

3. Keep your finger outside the trigger guard and on the receiver until beginning the shot.

4. Be sure of your target and its background.

Jim says that the class will be interactive, that he will invent scenarios and we will figure out how to respond. He walks over to my table, points to me, and says, "Here's this petite young lady with no protection," and pointing to the woman next to me, "and here's this woman with a black belt in karate, but you [meaning you, the students] are standing there and don't know any of this. You don't know that one is protectionless and the other can take care of herself in this situation."

Jim then pulls a knife out of his pocket, flips it open, walks down the center of the classroom, acting the part of an attacker, gleaming knife in hand. His voice rises. "I'm going to kill you! I'm going to effing rip you apart from effing limb to limb!" The man is a gifted actor. He paces up and down the center aisle so that each of us experiences him as a threat. He looks each student in the eye, then fires questions that come quick as shots.

"What are you gonna do? What's the word? No! Wrong word! Don't say *Kill*. Say *Stop him*. If you have an avenue of escape, you must use it. I'm thirty feet from you, threatening you with this knife, but you are next to the back door there. You can leave. But what if I'm moving toward you," he wields the knife, moving closer, "and there is no door? What about chairs, what about these tables? Use a table as shield. The knife can't go through the table. And verbalize. Even if you don't see anyone, someone might be watching. This is the Third Eye

Concept. Always verbalize. *Drop the effing knife!* That's what you have to say!"

Some of us rise to the challenge of Jim's teaching mode, jumping in fast with answers. Others retreat. His wild style makes me shy, and I find it difficult to think quickly and clearly in the midst of his dramas. I do not have the luxury of time to absorb what is happening. What a quandary for cops who must make split-second decisions during real dramas.

Jim uses all of us as characters in every story he enacts. This is good entertainment, but of course, entertainment is the least of it. After a few hours, I don't know how I can continue being so focused. It's hard to be part of his dramas for eight hours straight. At one point Jim points to me and says, "She's been raped and murdered . . ." I don't know what he says after that, because I am wondering why on earth I am even there in that moment. The moment passes.

To illustrate a new point, he looks at me and says, "You're out with your girlfriends at the bar. I'm sitting at the bar, and I walk over to you. I come on to you. You blow me off. I sit down, have another glass of courage, and come on to you again. You tell your girlfriends you want to leave. They're having a good time, laughing, relaxing. They persuade you to stay. You're uncomfortable but you stay. I leave the bar, go to the parking lot. The bar closes. They're cleaning up in there. You walk to your car alone. I'm waiting for you. You're alone because you came here in your own car. No one's around. I am in my pickup and drive over to you standing there. I get out, come on to you again. What are you gonna do?"

I gulp and say, "Draw my gun."

"Why?" he says.

"Well, there's no one around and I am feeling really threatened."

"What are you scared of?"

"I don't know," I say, "but the situation is threatening."

He is creating a scene which has gotten me completely shaky. "Say the word! Everyone's afraid to say the word! What are you afraid of?"

"Rape!"

"Right. That's the word. That's right. You are right to produce a gun in this situation, because of J-A-M: Jeopardy. Ability to cause serious bodily harm/death. Means. The means to do it. Thus, you can use deadly force to stop that from happening."

Then Jim says to a guy who looks sleepy, "Hey, come on. Wake up!"

"Just finished a twelve-hour shift," he answers.

"Why are you all here?" Jim asks. "Self-defense? Self-protection?"

Just about everyone raises their hand. I do too, but I do not say it's protection from grizzlies, or anything about Operation Berkshire. It is sobering to lay eyes on this room full of people, most of whom want to become armed citizens to protect themselves, their families, and their homes.

I have had a longtime fascination with *querencia*. *Querencia* is the invisible place in a bullring where the bull goes during a bullfight, his place of safety where he gathers strength and becomes fearless. I have always had an overdeveloped need for *querencia*, for sanctuary. The need to protect one's territory is common in humans and other animals.

One man does not raise his hand, the guy who just finished his twelve-hour shift. His chalky face is asymmetrical. "So why are you here?" Jim asks.

"I'm here to renew. Criminal record."

"Okay. Come see me at lunch break."

What is his story? Maybe he was imprisoned wrongly for years. Maybe his face is slanted because he was slapped around by other inmates.

Now Jim begins to tell us what it is really like if you shoot someone. "We live our lives based on TV. It gets people paranoid. It paints an untrue picture. Let's say you are an NRA member in good standing. You legally shoot someone while protecting yourself and others. You are not going to feel celebratory. You will be in a postshooting trauma. People will say accusatory things to you like 'Well, maybe you coulda done something different and not killed the guy.' Or, 'Good going! Yeah! Right on! You got that sonofabitch!' No. You are going to be vomiting. They don't show you this on TV. You will not be joyful. Get yourself to a hospital and tell them to treat you for stress. You can't know what it's like to have a shooting confrontation. The psychological effects are overwhelming. You are going to keep seeing that guy's face, his lungs filling with blood. You won't be able to get his face out of your mind."

Jim turns solemn. "Use your right to remain silent. Get a good criminal attorney. Don't make statements if you're emotionally upset—and you *will* be emotionally upset. It's an irreversible action." He continues, "There are three sides to every story. Yours, mine, and the truth." This man is no fool. He pauses. He lets this sink in. Then he announces it is time for our lunch break. "Be back in half an hour."

A bearded Englishman walks over to me and says, "You look very familiar." He owns an antique store in a nearby town.

"Why are you taking the class?" I ask.

"I guess I'm paranoid. I bought a house in West Virginia, and oddly enough, the previous owner left a cache of guns, which gave me the notion to learn to use them."

This British fellow and I drive to McDonald's, where we are joined by one of our classmates. He says that he is a Walmart store manager. "It is store policy for each manager to have a gun permit," he explains. Because he seems so awkward and odd, I later call Walmart headquarters to check this out, and learn that it is not true. Why has he made this up? Who are the other student shooters?

When we return to the classroom, I notice how each person moves, what they are wearing. Most of all, I wonder why they are here. One man in his early forties with a nice goofy smile wants to get a permit for target shooting. Another man, a real estate lawyer, deals with abandoned properties in local neighborhoods and wants to be armed as he prowls around these areas. When he mentions that he has a daughter in college, Jim moves to his next subject. "So . . . your daughter is shopping at the mall, big sales at Old Navy. She walks out to the parking lot in the dark. Make sure she has one of these, okay?"

He holds up a small canister. "Chemical aerosol for self-defense is great stuff. The best. Mace, pepper spray, tear gas. Make sure your daughter has it, make sure your girlfriend has it, *and* your wife. It doesn't work on ten to twelve percent of the population. You have to be careful that the person you are spraying doesn't grab it and use it on you. There are three types: cone mist, which is affected by how the wind is blowing, which is not good, foam, and stream aerosol."

Jim's favorite is stream aerosol because you can spray it from a distance. He suggests testing a chemical weapon on yourself because it may end up used back on you.

Jim talks about the rise in sexual crimes at the University of Massachusetts and the fact that the university does not allow chemical weapons. He says that if he had a daughter, he would give her some anyway. "It is crazy not to allow people to defend themselves in light of what's happening there." He stresses that each person has to weigh each situation and in that one he would break the law.

After the chemical weapons lesson, we all troop down the hall to the teaching range, where paper targets hang on wooden stilts; the shape suggests a person pointing a gun at you, the student shooter. Jim tells us each to choose a partner. I team up with a young black man with snazzy white sneaker-type shoes. Jim gives strict instructions on how to handle the gun, load it, and shoot it.

"Low ready," he says. That's the position you take with the muzzle of the gun pointing downrange and low. "Load. One Shot. Two Shots. Five Shots. Ten shots. Step back."

My partner and I take turns shooting the target. As the sensation of power rises to consciousness, I feel surprisingly comfortable and good. Each of us tries to outdo the other as we shoot, and we joke about whose bullet hits the bullseye more often. With potential for becoming a good shot, I want to shoot more.

Later, we return to the classroom and Jim talks about home invasions. "What if someone threatens you with deadly force in your house? Your house is your castle. You do not have to flee your house. But you should have a safe spot in your house, and everyone living there should know where it is. You need a phone, a flashlight, a lock on the door, and a gun—maybe a twenty-gauge pump shotgun. If you hear someone break in, what do you do? Verbalize. Yell, 'Please leave my home. I've called the police. I've got a gun.' Your gun should be two walking steps from your bed, not in the nightstand next to your bed." Jim reads us newspaper accounts of mix-ups when people were half-asleep. One man reached for his asthma inhaler and shot himself in the mouth.

Jim continues. "Or you pull into your driveway. You see a guy leaving from a side door, carrying who knows what. He's leaving. He is no threat to you or your family. You cannot pull a gun on him, no matter what he has taken."

It is now test time. I am exhausted. Jim passes out the test. By now he has told us all the questions and answers. Some of us have taken notes, which we can keep out during the test. Under these conditions, anyone can pass it. Jim leaves the room. When he returns, he corrects the papers. Everyone has passed. In a few minutes, we will all have our certificates. The day is over, we say goodbye, and I drive home to the Berkshires.

After that long Smith and Wesson day, the shooting students knew a lot about the legalities and safety of handgun use: locked containers, trigger locks, guns well-hidden, firearms and alcohol do not mix. But except for a few basics, none of us learned how to shoot. Years ago, I had spent many afternoons preparing for my driving test, and this was much easier. Even before I got my certificate to apply for a permit, I was appalled at how easy it was to get a gun legally, and I still am.

The following week, I set out for the police station to apply for a gun permit. There was a chill in the air, snow predicted for the next day. I walked up through the basketball courts, past the red plastic jungle gym, and noticed the plastic vehicle with a toy sign Ambulance affixed to it. How odd to have a sign implying calamity in a children's playground. I rehearsed what I would say to the chief of police when he interviewed me. Jim had said that when we applied for a Class A Unrestricted Permit, we would have to make a strong case for why we needed a handgun for self-protection more than the average citizen. Because I took the course to qualify, I wanted to apply.

"Why do you need this type of permit?" he would ask.

"I'm an avid hiker," I would reply. Then I would tell him my scary bear story. No, I would not say *avid*. I have never used the word *avid*. I would say, "I like to hike, and this past summer in Alaska I became really afraid of bears. I need a handgun for self-defense in the woods." I would act like I'm a major hiker, which I am not. I would not talk about Operation Berkshire, my writing project.

In a bit of fog, I wandered into Town Hall, then realized it was the wrong place. So down the hill I went, to the police station. Gun permit forms were piled up in a big bin in the lobby. I picked one up and a kind woman led me through the process of filling out the application. Then she helped me look up addresses for my two references. Jim had said the police just stash your references in your file. They dig them out only if you get yourself into trouble.

The application asked for hair color, eye color, height, weight, and build. *Build*? I left it blank. Then I was fingerprinted for the first time since I was born. The police would check to see if I had a criminal record, if I had ever been admitted to a mental hospital, and if there were any disqualifiers on my record. For example, if I had ever been treated for alcohol or drug abuse, I could not get a gun permit.

I was becoming apprehensive, waiting for my interview. When I handed in the application, the woman took a photograph of me, to be laminated onto the permit. She said, "You'll be hearing in about two weeks."

"Don't I have to be interviewed by Chief Moss?"

"Oh no, there are way too many people applying for permits now. We don't have time for interviews."

No interview? Getting a permit was even easier than I had believed. I could get a gun license—Class A Unrestricted—allowing me to carry concealed weapons, with ease. To obtain a certificate for this permit, I had spent less than an hour with my classmates in the shooting range. I had taken a written test that everyone passed. And now there would be no interview. What extremely bad news for the United States of America.

I thanked the woman and trudged home. When evening came, I put on a B. B. King CD and fixed dinner. As my husband Paul and I sat down to our fish chowder, he half-joked, "What could be nicer. You're protecting our home." Less than two weeks later, my gun permit arrived in the mail.

Clay and I made a plan to go shooting every week. Looking for a closer shooting range, we went to check out a local Sportsmen's Club.

When we stopped at the State Police Barracks to get directions, a cop asked why we were going there. "We are pistol shooters and have been driving the hour over to Smith and Wesson and want to check out a local range," answered Clay.

The cop, drawing a map for us, said, "Good. Good. We need people like you, especially, you know, with all the New Yorkers coming around. I saw this great bumper sticker down at the Cape. *If it's tourist season, why can't we shoot them?*"

My stomach turned.

We left and drove past the hardware store, the supermarket, the auto mechanic shop, and up a long curving hill. At the end of a dirt road was the Sportsmen's Club, with a bunch of pickups in the parking lot. Inside was a long low-ceilinged room with archery targets at one end and a bar at the other, where a few men sat, some clean-cut, some not. A friendly fellow led us down to the basement. The shooting range was dirty, low-lit, and makeshift. There were a few fans for ventilation and a padlock on the door. A hole was cut into the wall to slip in your $2.00 shooting fee. No one oversaw the raunchy range. In other words, you come here, go downstairs, unlock the padlock, turn on the lights, turn on the fans, slide your money into the hole, press the button that sends your target to the distance you want it, and start shooting. As we walked back upstairs, the fellow remarked, "All the housewives come down and take the course for their permit and then you never see them again." As we left, Clay and I planned never to go back.

Yesterday, driving over to Smith and Wesson with Clay, I called him my *shooting buddy*, then changed it to *shooting teacher*.

"I'm your shooting *sensei*," he said in his Southern drawl. He sees shooting as a martial art with all the discipline, focus, and meditative activity such undertakings require. Later I looked up *sensei*.

Sensei: *sen* means "before," *sei* means "life, birth, living or lived." Thus, a *sensei* is someone who has experienced something before you. He has walked the path you are planning to follow, he can tell you what to do.

Clay loved the role of guide. He felt a responsibility to pass his knowledge along to someone else. He was my Virgil in this inferno-tainted endeavor.

⁂

We arrive at the range, register, show our gun permits, and buy ammunition. We heap all our stuff—his gun box, my backpack, his attaché case, our big down jackets—on a plastic chair outside the shop, which sells Smith and Wesson logoed mugs, key rings, clothes, and of course guns. We suit up for shooting and go down to the nearly empty range. We each have our own shooting stall.

Clay is saying, "You've gotta relax. It's not very hard to do well at this. Focus on each little step of getting the gun ready, gripping it, standing, and then when you've done it all, just stand there and shoot. Don't try too hard."

The gun I'm shooting is Clay's Ruger .22 caliber target pistol, with a bull barrel and grips like a .45. Clay calls it a paper punch, because with a target-shooting gun, you make holes in paper. But it is a deadly weapon.

Clay asks me to repeat the steps over and over. Push the lower button in to release the magazine. When the magazine slides out, hold it in your left hand and insert the ammo. One at a time, pop five bullets into the magazine with your right hand. Each bullet is called a *round*. Clay loads only five rounds at a time, although the magazine holds ten, to keep track of what he has already shot. Each time you raise your gun, you shoot a string of five rounds.

The ammo comes in a small orange plastic box with five bullets per row. You slide the box's cover back, pop the row of bullets onto the ledge of your cubby, load them into the magazine. Find a good stance. Then, holding the gun with your right hand, insert the magazine into the grip. Slide the upper button down to release the slide, and put your right hand around the grip, never putting your index finger on the trigger—that's basic. Put your left hand around your right hand, covering it. Both thumbs should hang there together, parallel, not doing anything. You have this good firm grip, gripping harder with your left hand. Loosen up your body, wiggle it, shake out the tension. It is important for all these steps to feel natural. Meanwhile, you're excited and nervous. You're about to shoot.

Let's see. I have found my nice stance, slightly wide, facing the range, with a slight tilt toward the right. My right foot goes slightly back. With a little bend in my elbows, I raise the gun with both hands and line up the sights, front and rear. Clay reminds me not to worry about hitting the target. "It's irrelevant." But I want to hit the target. I aim the gun and slowly shoot five rounds, my string. This is slow-fire shooting, not *bangbangbangbangbang*—that's rapid-fire—but *bang*, pause, *bang*, pause, *bang*, pause, *bang*, pause, *bang*.

While I am shooting, shells fly all over the place, hitting the shield over my glasses, bouncing off the tip of my cap, hitting me on the head. The nitroglycerin smell released into the air goes to my head. The shooting is not exactly hypnotic, but it is very satisfying.

Clay says I should have my own target pistol, in order to get to really know the particular gun's grip, trigger, sights. I need to know my gun like I know my camera, an intimate possession that feels like an extension of my arm. As long as I borrow or rent a gun, that kind of relationship won't evolve. Paul has been asking whether I am going to get a gun.

"Don't worry, I'm so far away from that," I say. But at this moment, tearful to have traveled so far, I realize I have come closer to crossing into this fresh territory.

Now that I have my gun license, now that I have spent my long day at Smith and Wesson, now that I have been able to talk about my shooting to men on the right and wrong sides of the law, now that I've told friends and family about all this and heard their multitudinous reactions, now that I have had the sensation of shooting a pistol, now that I have joked about using my government-issued gun permit at the airport—what now? Am I going to own a gun?

Epilogue

Gun violence in the United States has become commonplace in the twenty years since I learned to shoot. Not a day goes by that there isn't a mass shooting. Shootings are the largest cause of childhood death. Just last week, students at the University of Virginia were gunned down, people out for a night of fun in Colorado were gunned down, and workers at a Walmart were gunned down by a coworker. Sandy Hook happened ten years ago and after all the weekly sympathies and prayers, our country still chooses guns over children. Even though most Americans want strong gun control measures, up to now our faulty political system has made this impossible.

I doubt I would have learned to shoot in today's violent climate. But if I had, I wonder if I would have been open to experiencing the elemental appeal of shooting—the pleasure of the focus, the sensuousness, the primal physical thrill.

Although I considered buying a gun, I never did buy one. I was swayed by my husband's opposition to the idea. But even now with such runaway gun violence, I can imagine owning a gun. If I had to defend myself or a beloved against a mortal threat, I would use it.

Writing these words is hard and sad because I'd give anything for all the guns in the world to be turned into pruning hooks and ploughshares.

Befriend Only to Betray

If you and I don't know each other, someone I know knows you. That's how it is in Berkshire County on the far western edge of Massachusetts, and that's how it was in the dingy basement room of the county courthouse one summer morning in 2000. I was there with other local residents who had been called for jury duty. Jury duty is always an interruption, but this time, because I had been traveling far from home giving readings from my new poetry book, I welcomed being with familiar folks. I had been missing my friends and neighbors.

Hours passed with no word about who was going to serve. We weren't allowed to leave the stuffy room, so some of us began to complain about the jury selection process. Then, as we chewed jelly donuts and drank bad coffee, one woman mentioned that a bear had wrestled her bird feeder to the ground the night before. A man said he had read that a bear had killed a woman hiking in the Smokies the week before. With the increase of the black bear population, bears were on everyone's mind.

I asked if anyone recalled anything about a black bear poaching investigation that I vaguely remembered. Soon we were all sharing fragmented memories of an event that had happened over a decade earlier. Intrigued, I was full of questions. One fellow suggested I call the environmental law officer from the next town, who had supervised the investigation.

I wanted to know more before making that call. After no luck searching the web, I went to the library to look for newspaper articles on the microfiche machine. The first story I found, from the *Berkshire Eagle* of January 25, 1989, startled me.

> A five-state 2½ year sting operation intended to hobble a bustling black-market trade in wildlife meat, skins and organs climaxed yesterday with the arrest of 23 suspected poachers and accomplices.
>
> The covert investigation, in which two officers worked undercover and side by side with several alleged outlaws, revealed the existence of a major underground industry in which black bears are killed for their gallbladders, which are dried, reduced to powder, and sold in the Orient as an aphrodisiac. . . .

Economic need, a desire for adventure, a pleasure in the kill, even revenge may cause poachers to hunt bears for their gallbladders, elephants for their tusks, or rhinos for their horns. In Africa today elephants and rhinos are severely threatened by widespread poaching. In Korea black bears are nearly extinct because of poaching. Here in my own backyard, a large bear-poaching ring had flourished.

Stories of men and bears are timeless. They have captivated humans with their power since the beginning of recorded history. From the bear on the walls of the Lascaux Caves in France, painted some twenty thousand years ago, to stories in yesterday's newspapers, bears fascinate. In a crowd of people today, just say the word *bear*, and everyone vies to tell their own bear story.

The more I learned about Operation Berkshire, the more I wanted to learn. As a woman writer entering a man's domain, I suspected I would be challenged. I was following my curiosity, with no idea where it would lead. A series of poems? A full-fledged writing project? A dead end?

Eventually I interviewed all the main players, those on the

right side of the law and those on the wrong. The more men I spoke with, the more elusive and various truth became. *Rashomon* was alive and well in Operation Berkshire, truth as faceted as a fine diamond. I ended up feeling compelled to tell the story of the investigation and the men involved.

During that summer, I visited Lieutenant Tom Kasprzak, the supervising environmental officer of the operation, numerous times, recording our conversations. When I first drove to meet him, weeks of humidity had been gathering. The sky was overcast, the air heavy. Lush trees hovered over the road. Ascending a hill, I arrived at his house in the woods. A big state police car was parked in the driveway.

A tall, dark-haired man with smart, sparkling eyes greeted me. We sat in his wood-paneled dining room, with windows looking out to the forest and lots of blooming mountain laurel. He had prepared for our meeting by heaping the table with scrapbooks, search warrants, the police report, a dried bear gallbladder, videotapes, and magazine articles. The sheer amount of stuff intimidated me. For over three hours, with great aplomb, Tom relayed his victories, disappointments, and musings.

He outlined the basis of undercover work. "*You befriend only to betray*. We looked at the boys as friends in a phony context, with the ultimate mindset that we are going to betray you. We are going to expose you. Then arrests can be made.

"It was addictive being inside, seeing how they think. We're learning about a subculture, the psyche of a subculture. We're not sure what we have, but we know it keeps getting bigger and bigger."

Ultimately, Operation Berkshire resulted in the arrests of twenty-three individuals, charged with 1,100 counts of illegal possession and commerce of wildlife. Three men received sixty-day jail sentences. The penalties were substantially less than they would have been if not for bitter conflicts between the state and the federal agents. One result of the operation was the Northeast Conservation Law Enforcement Compact, which provides for interstate cooperation in enforcing environmental laws and offers mutual aid and assistance.

With summer in full swing in the culture-filled Berkshires, I spent day after day transcribing the tapes of my talks with Tom. The slow process of transcription drew me deeper into the story. As a steady stream of tourists arrived to watch dance performances at Jacob's Pillow or listen to music at Tanglewood, I was listening to Tom give an overview of how Operation Berkshire came about and unfolded. He described what it was like for him and for the undercover agents, Jack and Steve, who were always nervous the poachers would unmask them. There were close calls.

One night Jack and Steve were in a pickup truck in New Hampshire, driving up a desolate mountain road on a bear hunt. Another truckful of poachers drove up next to them, and the men passed beers back and forth from one truck to the other. Steve turned on his body wire, which set off a radar detector. The poachers looked around for cops. One said, "There's never cops on this road. What's goin' on?" Steve was able to turn off the body wire, and the radar detector went silent. After that, they stopped using the body wire.

"How dangerous do you think it really was, Tom?" I asked.

Almost whispering, he said, "They were way out in the dark woods with those guys."

I was reminded of my childhood love of frightening fairy tales. Their foreboding settings were peopled with villains and heroes who took long dark walks through big dark forests. There was violence. I was afraid of the dark and wouldn't go to sleep unless my mother read me fairy tales. To hear about unmediated good and evil, with no shades of gray, satisfied me and perhaps helped me make some sense of the huge world.

Operation Berkshire contained some of the same elements as

fairy tales. Violence was visited upon beasts deep in the forest. Their body parts served as a magic potion, the heart of the struggle between heroes and villains. It was only after I met the men involved in the operation that shades of gray fell over the forces of good and evil, the true story far more complex than any fairy tale.

That summer, whatever I was doing made me think about the investigation. It was alchemy—much of what I did or saw was stimulus for the work. This chemistry had happened to me during other writing projects. When it occurred, nearly everything became useful.

The way Tom told the story made it sound as if he had faced down the rogue hunters just the day before. What were the other players like? I decided to call one of the poachers who lived nearby.

As I dressed to go meet Al the next week, my pink toenail polish seemed wrong, so I wiped it off. Look neutral, I thought, look sort of pretty but not very, look regular and comfortable. So on went my white-and-beige-striped cotton pants and a slogan-less white T-shirt.

I pulled up to Al's house and the slaughterhouse where he made his legal living. There was a spiffy fishing boat hooked to the back of a blue-gray pickup, and assorted other vehicles. Al, a bit portly, walked toward my car hesitantly.

"Hi, I'm Karen." I extended my hand. He wore a tilted red baseball cap, jeans, sneakers, a faded dark green polo shirt, glasses, several chins, and a slow manner.

"Hi. I have a lot of questions for you," he said.

"I'm sure you do, I don't blame you."

"Why do you want to talk to me?" Al asked. "I told people you were coming over, and every last one said that I'm crazy to talk to you. Last night a friend of mine, a cop, was here. He said, 'You're crazy!' You might twist something I say and I'd end up getting in trouble again."

"Yeah," I answered, "I was wondering why you'd talk to me

103

too. One of my first questions was going to be how you could trust anyone after what happened. So why are you talking to me?"

Al motioned me toward a freestanding screened-in porch on the lawn, with unmatching aluminum lawn chairs inside. We sat down.

"Well, I may be gullible," he began, "well, I *am* gullible, but I like to help people. If someone comes in here and they want something, I like to help them." And then Al talked and talked, giving voice to his haunting experience.

He described the first time he took the undercover agents to New Hampshire to go bear hunting with his pal Carl. Carl shot a bear, cut it open, and removed the gallbladder. Leaving the bear remains scattered in the woods, he brought the bear gall back to his house and placed it on his kitchen table.

Al explained, "Steve and Jack said they were going to buy it. That's how the galls got goin'."

When he came to the story of the takedown and his arrest, Al's face turned deep red and his body shook.

"It was six o'clock in the morning. Snow. I was up and I saw lights flashing like someone was driving in the yard. I didn't know what was going on. I had a bunch of pigs, thought maybe they got out of the pens. Then I opened the door and the federal wardens with search warrants come in and made me sit down. I didn't know what was goin' on. What went wrong? What did I do wrong? There were sixteen wardens in my house here! Then the whole place was surrounded here. Television cameras out in the yard."

The story mushroomed in the media. "It went from two bear to three bear to three hundred bear. How this created so fast—unbelievable—the radio, the paper. All these phone calls were comin' in. My whole family should be burnt to the ground, and the house too! I should be hung up and skun alive!

"We don't hear from Steve and Jack. Where are these guys

now? Carl and I figured, if they were involved in it, they'd be arrested and be calling us. Now we're startin' to put two and two together. 'I betcha' Steve and Jack were undercovers, we were sayin'.'"

During the takedown, twenty-three men were arrested in five different states at the same moment early one winter morning.

On this sweltering afternoon, Al's torrent of words eventually slowed. Welcoming a break from the intense conversation, we chatted for a few minutes about local news. Al seemed to be wondering about me, then blurted, "What do you get out of doing this?"

"I don't know. It's just a deeply interesting story to me. And all the issues of morality and betrayal and trust, they're as old as—I mean, as long as people have existed, those are things they have dealt with. It's a story that brings all that up. I really want to talk to the undercover guys and ask them what it felt like to be lying all the time."

"That is what bothers me," Al said. "Just about everything else I can let go. I still have nightmares all the time about it."

As far as Al was concerned, he was a good man at heart, always ready to help whoever came along. He recognized that this characteristic sometimes got him into trouble. He felt he had been victimized by what he called "the system," which had been unfair to him.

Soon afterward, still reeling from our talk, I was visiting New York City. In Chinatown, I popped in and out of a few Asian apothecaries, inquiring about bear galls. "Medicine for stomach?" I had to gather my courage. This did not come naturally to me. "Herb for lovemaking?" No one seemed to understand what I was saying. I looked over the dried seahorses, soaps, snakeskins, bones, herbs lined up in rows of clear glass jars. I persisted with my questions, but no luck.

I was out of place in these shops, just as I was out of place working on the Operation Berkshire project. A poet? A woman? But I liked how unexpected it was to find myself sitting next to Al in front of his slaughterhouse exchanging questions. And I liked finding myself in a Chinese apothecary, inquiring about bear gallbladders. One pleasure of being a writer is that you can explore anything.

A few months later, ready for an infusion of fresh information, I called Jack Dickman, one of the undercover agents. Jack had had a brain aneurysm after Operation Berkshire.

"Perfect," he said, "meeting at noontime would be perfect."

On the appointed day, I dressed for our interview, first trying on my white linen sheath with buttons down the front and a V neckline. Then I thought, *No, wearing white is symbolically all wrong*, so I switched to a beige version of the sheath.

My mind was blank as I drove to Westboro to meet him at the offices of the Massachusetts Environmental Police. I pulled up to a rambling Victorian house—odd for an official building. Crowds of uniformed men stood around chatting, leaning against trees, leaning against pickups. A retirement party for one of the beloved cops was in full swing.

I found my way up a flight of creaky wooden stairs, passing more officially dressed men, guns on most hips. I felt like a spy, a probing observer in an unfamiliar land. I found the receptionist.

"Is Jack Dickman here?" I asked.

She looked out the large old window. "Oh! There he is outside. I'll go get him."

I glanced out the window. He was fiftyish, thin and short with a cane. One of the few men not in uniform, he wore a green sweatshirt and a green baseball cap and was chatting with several cops.

He suggested that we find a place upstairs to talk. We sat in a tiny decorless office, facing each other across a vast drab metal desk. Two large dirty windows stayed shut in the stifling autumn heat.

As I took my tape recorder from my purse, Jack grinned. "That looks familiar." When he was undercover, he said, he wore heavy army camouflage with big pockets where he hid his tape recorder.

"It was incredibly brave what you did, putting yourself in the position you put yourself in, going undercover and all," I began. I'd ask a question and Jack would mumble a word, rarely elaborating, but a few times he looked straight into my eyes and said what he was going to say with twinkling animation, as if doors were opening.

"The story was that me and Steve were friends from the service. Vietnam. I could talk that game. Steve was never there, but in '70 I was."

Jack told me about going to undercover school in Georgia. They had to learn how to act in order to gain entry into the poachers' circle. No matter how deeply they infiltrated the poachers' lives, they had to stay focused on their mission so they could make arrests for these crimes.

"What was that like for you, Jack?" I asked.

He grunted, laughed a little, then said slowly, in a low voice, "Kinda nasty thing to do, ain't it. Absolutely, you gotta stay positive as an undercover. Keep it focused. You gotta stay in touch with yourself, that what you're doin' is what you're supposed to be doin' and what they're doin' is absolutely wrong. You gotta put an end to their doin' of it."

By the time Operation Berkshire had been going on for over a year, a brisk business was underway between the hunters and their Asian customers, with Jack and Steve as the go-betweens. The sale of hundreds of bear galls, bear paws, deer antlers in velvet, saddles of venison, cougar skins, and arctic foxes financially supported the operation.

For Jack, the worst day was a bear hunt on which Carl shot some bear cubs. It was the most upsetting thing he ever saw the poachers do. He muttered something about how awful the sound of a wounded cub was. Tom had shown me the videotape Jack made, and it was horrifying.

"I was filming it. Right there. Feeling angry. Wished we could have done something at the time, but it was just the two of us and everybody had guns. We were way out up by the Canadian/ Maine border, definitely way out in the woods."

Jack paused. "I was getting pretty tense near the end. They were sorta catching on that something was up. Some guy from Maine told Carl he thought we were federal agents. Made me think we'd better wind it up."

Jack's stories made the danger palpable. The stress was extreme. Steve, Tom, and the second supervisor, Larry Johnson, worried about the toll it was taking on Jack. In retrospect, they wondered whether his subsequent brain aneurysm was related to the anxiety.

When I questioned Jack further about the danger, his complex feelings about fear and bravery showed on his taut face. "We didn't really feel our lives were in danger. Well, maybe we did. Because near the end we carried guns for personal protection. Made us feel a little safer, more secure. I wasn't scared. We were definitely way out in the woods."

I wanted to understand Jack better. I also suspected that I couldn't fully understand any of these men unless I inhabited their world more. Hesitantly, I decided to learn to shoot, and spent months taking lessons at Smith and Wesson. I was surprised how much I liked it: the gun's kick, the gun's bang, the intoxicating odor as the bullets fired. And I was good at it. But I was disturbed as never before by the sheer power of guns. Although I believe learning to shoot deepened my grasp of these men, I also wonder whether I was trying to gain a sense of mastery over what was steadily becoming a darker journey.

One of the last men I interviewed was Carl, the poacher from New Hampshire. By then, I had gathered that he had a frightening sadistic side, but I was committed to exploring the many-sided story of Operation Berkshire thoroughly. I had to deal with my fears.

The call to Carl was the hardest to make. I introduced myself and said I was a poet. Who would be threatened by a poet?

"Good!" he replied. There was nothing menacing in his energetic voice. He said he was coming to the Berkshires the next week to hunt with Al and would call me.

There was an icy nor'easter the day we were to meet. I was shoveling layers of wet snow off my deck when the phone rang.

"I'll be looking for you in the McDonald's parking lot in forty-five minutes," he said. "I'll be in a burnt orange Chevy pickup."

I got in my car and headed to nearby Great Barrington. Meeting at McDonald's was perfect, no danger there. I saw his truck. A creepy, sinewy man stood by the door smoking.

"Carl?"

"Hello," he said, and I saw that it wasn't Carl as I noticed *Jim* embroidered in white script on his workshirt. Then a smiling fellow came out of the restaurant, with grayish blond medium-length hair, wire-rimmed glasses, and a plaid flannel shirt tucked into his corduroys. We shook hands and Carl led me back inside and over to a booth.

Once we were seated, he leaned forward, his posture turning aggressive as he fixed his eyes on mine. He'd make a point, glare at me, then loudly repeat, "Do you understand what I am saying? Do you understand what I am saying?"

I nodded, trying to stay calm.

"What do you perceive me as doin' here today? You tell me!

What am I doin' with you here today? I just saved you a two-hundred-and-fifty-mile trip. Did I or did I not? This is what I was doin' with these people here, when I brought galls down here and sold them to them. I saved you a trip. I saved them people a trip."

When Carl and I had arranged our meeting, he said we would talk for twenty minutes, but we spoke for over an hour. Carl expounded on the sensations of the hunt. "You know what happens, you get an adrenaline pump. Some bears, they didn't intimidate me, but I give them some space. Their hair was up and you could see it in their eyes. Just like a guy in a barroom. Loudmouths. Just like the old gunfighter."

Finally, we walked out to the snowy parking lot. We had arranged a second meeting, in the spring in New Hampshire. Carl said, "You must be forty-five, fifty."

I said, "No. I'm almost sixty."

He said, "You are doin' good!" What a charmer. What woman wouldn't like this flattery? His warmth, animation, and directness combined with his sadism was perplexing. I felt like a hunter walking deep into the forest of knowledge to find god knows what.

Before I made the New Hampshire trip, I called Tom to tell him I was going to interview Carl again. Did he have any questions he wanted me to ask?

"Yes. Why, in all the videotapes of the bear hunts, why is he always closest to the bloodiest worst stuff? The stabbing, the sadistic killing? And his voice is always the primary voice-over?" I told Tom to send up a posse for me if I didn't return home in a couple of days, half-joking.

On the way to Carl's house, I got off the highway and found a diner in some little town. A wooden sign hung over the cash register: Where Friendly People Meet. Plastic Swedish ivy plants decorated each table. Specials on the board: Roast Pork with Real

Mash Potato and Veggie, Chicken Parm on H.R. with Chips. The sound of frying was loud and grating.

During the five-hour drive, showers alternated with sunshine. Magnolias and crab apples were in bloom, and new leaves were about to burst. Finally I arrived at the Wolfeboro Inn, overlooking a large lake. My room had two rose brocade wing chairs and fine polished furniture. I hoped its luxury would calm my agitated mind. I walked to a restaurant for dinner, where I made a list of questions for Carl. Back in my room, I turned on the TV and got lost in some dumb program.

Carl and I had planned to meet at 8:30 the next morning at his garage/office, the hub of his logging business. I packed up and went down to the hotel restaurant for breakfast. Eggs Benedict hit the spot. Then I called Carl to say I was on my way.

Carl greeted me warmly. We sat down on black faux-leather chairs. Family photos and paintings hung on the rough wood-paneled walls: young Carl with a .22; a painting of Carl on the Iditarod Trail in front of a shack with two grizzlies added; an arrow-shaped metal sign that said Carl's Way or No Way.

Carl wore rimless sunglasses, a navy chamois shirt, and dungarees. I was glad to see him, and it seemed mutual. He picked a baseball cap off a mounted deer head whose antlers served as a hat rack. He told me the limited-edition cap was a collector's item, then presented it to me. He began to talk.

When I asked him if he ever hunted bears with the express purpose of cutting out their gallbladders, Carl seemed insulted. "No, no. We never hunted for galls. Ever. We never, ever went gall hunting. Never. See, I got a clear, clear conscience about it, you know what I mean? I got a very clear conscience about it. Don't bother me a bit. I would not kill them animals unless there was a reason. Just go out and wanting to kill 'em—I don't do that."

Carl appeared to believe what he was saying, but I didn't. I knew too much.

After a while, he wanted to show me his camp up the mountain on a small lake, so we got in his pickup, stopped at his newly built house, where I met his wife, and proceeded up the winding dirt road.

He launched into a spirited discussion about how new laws had been passed in New Hampshire because of his actions, how the statute of limitations on hunting violations had been extended from ninety days to three years.

"You sound kind of proud," I said.

"Well, yeah! Know what I mean. Not too many guys have laws made over them. You understand?"

Carl, like the other men I had interviewed, had many stories he was intent on telling. "I did crazy stuff, I'll tell you, dear, stuff that I don't need repeated. I mean I really don't want to divulge some of it," he said. He talked emotionally about his family's history, his youth, and his children. Then he said, "Have you seen me on *National Geographic*, right there on TV? I was on *National Geographic Explorer*, with a knife, that bear coming down the tree. That was when I was wild and crazy. Not a big deal. I killed two of them. I killed another one with a knife too, another small bear like that, probably you're talkin' a sixty-pound bear. But they still can fight you pretty good, or cut you, like a pit bull getting after you. Did you see that videotape? Did you see me hitting the bear with the knife?"

"Yes, and I'm trying to piece together these two people, you in the video and you as a family man. It's a little hard." His stories were confounding and contradictory. For sure, he was a lively, enthusiastic charmer, but his dark side was untouchable, as if it had an impermeable shell covering it.

As I was getting ready to leave, Carl blurted out, "You coming up here two hundred miles to see me, and then venturing up to my camp and my house with me. You didn't know whether my wife was around. Especially with what the cops have told you about me, what a no-good sonofabitch I am. You already got your mind poisoned before you ever talked to me."

I said, "Yes and no. Poisoned in one way, but not poisoned at all in another way." Having seen the videotape surely had a huge effect, but my curiosity about other sides of him kept me slightly open.

"We talked together half the day, and you must've trusted me a little bit to come up."

I told him that on my drive north, it had occurred to me that I didn't know what I would do if he suggested going to his camp but decided to trust my judgment at the time. I said I wanted to be brave but not stupid, and then I mentioned that I had written a series of poems about bears. Carl wanted to read them, so I opened my purse and gave him the poems. We shook hands, and I got in my car to drive the five hours home. It was late in the day, but the sun still illuminated the new green on the trees. The light was amazing. Every once in a while the sky turned black and it poured.

⁂

"Sweetie pie?" my husband calls as he walks through the door of our house. He's looking for me. I'm sitting in the living room, drinking a glass of wine and glancing at the newspaper. I've been out in my office all day, writing.

He comes into the living room holding a plastic bag. "I visited Ray this afternoon, and guess what. He gave me some bear meat. A friend of his shot it, and he fixed it pot-roast style for dinner last night. He said it was good."

As I have finally accumulated all the material to begin this story, as I finally have a hold on it, this wonderful coincidence comes about. I have never seen bear meat, but there is a bag of it in my refrigerator. Some primitive cultures eat their enemies for strength, and some eat their loved ones out of respect. Tonight we will eat bear.

Notes

"BOOM: A Vaccine Story"

The quotations on pages 3 and 4 regarding the sending of dimes to the White House are quoted in Tony Gould, *A Summer Plague: Polio and Its Survivors* (New Haven, CT: Yale University Press, 1995), 74.

The newspaper quotation on page 4 was reprinted in Victor Cohn, *Four Billion Dimes* (Minneapolis, MN: Minneapolis Star and Tribune, 1955), 9.

"Polio Boulevard"

The FDR quotations on page 12 are recorded in Frank Freidel, *Franklin D. Roosevelt: The Ordeal* (New York: Little, Brown, and Company, 1954), 98.

FDR's quotation regarding Orson Welles on page 12 is recorded on FDR on Lying: Hiding a Disability, *American Experience*, PBS, https://www.pbs.org/wgbh/americanexperience/features/presidents-lying/.

The quotation from Hugh Gallagher on page 13 is from American Experience: FDR, written and produced by David Grubin, aired May 12, 2008, on PBS, transcript, https://www.pbs.org/wgbh/americanexperience/films/fdr/?feature_filter=All&page=2#transcript.

The quotation from FDR about flying on page 14 is from "Affectionately Yours, F.D.R." Franklin D. Roosevelt's Long-Lost Letters to Daisy Suckley, Roosevelt House, Hunter College, http://www.roosevelthouse.hunter.cuny.edu/exhibits/affectionately-fdr/.

The quotation beginning "[My father and the president]" on page 15 is from Lady Mary Soames, *American Experience: FDR*. PBS. Air date: 1994.

"Ship Ahoy: FDR's Houseboat Years"

The two quotes from FDR's log on page 18 is from Elliott Roosevelt and James Brough, *The Roosevelts of Hyde Park: An Untold Story* (New York: G. P. Putnam's Sons, 1973), 160.

The image of a sailboat drawn by FDR as a child on page 19 is courtesy of the Franklin D. Roosevelt Presidential Library.

The *New York Times* article quoted on page 19 is "Franklin D. Roosevelt Better" (*New York Times*, August 28, 1921.

The quotations of FDR's letter to his mother on pages 19 and 20 is from Elliott Roosevelt, ed. *F.D.R.—His Personal Letters (Early Years; 1905–1928)*, vol. 2 (New York: Duell, Sloan, and Pearce, 1947), 53

The quotation of Eleanor Roosevelt's reaction to the *Weona* on page 20 is from Jean Edward Smith, *FDR* (New York: Random House Reprint, 2008), 203.

The quotation of Louis Howe on page 20 is from Donald S. Carmichael, *An Introduction to the Log of the Larooco—Being Chiefly the Correspondence of Franklin D. Roosevelt and John S. Lawrence* (Hyde Park: manuscript of FDR Archives, 1948), 4.

The quotation from FDR beginning "What I am looking for" on page 21 is from Elliott Roosevelt and James Brough, *The Roosevelts of Hyde Park: An Untold Story* (New York: G. P. Putnam's Sons, 1973), 159.

The quotation from FDR beginning "The owner is" on page 21 is from Carmichael, 7.

The quotation from FDR beginning "It has been suggested" on page 21 is from Carmichael, 14.

The quotation from Lawrence beginning "How would you like" on page 21 is from Carmichael, 23.

The memo reproduced on pages 21 and 22 is from Carmichael, 20–21.

The letter from FDR to Lawrence quoted on pages 22 and 23 is from Carmichael, 25.

The letter from FDR to his doctor on page 23 is from Roosevelt and Brough, 196.

The quotation that begins "'But aren't you'" on page 24 is from Hazel Rowley, *Franklin and Eleanor: An Extraordinary Marriage* (New York: Farrar, Straus, And Giroux, 2010), 130.

The quotation from FDR's letter to his daughter Anna on page 24 is from Roosevelt, ed., 582.

FDR's inscription to Marion on page 25 is from Kenneth S. Davis, *invincible Summer: An Intimate Portrait of the Roosevelts, Based on the Recollections of Marion Dickerman* (New York: Atheneum, 1974), 50.

The quotation from Missy LeHand on page 25 is from Jan Pottker, *Sara and Eleanor* (New York: St. Martins Griffin, 2005), 230.

The quotation from FDR on pages 25 and 26 that begins "The water put me" is from Roosevelt and Brough, 162.

The quotation from FDR on page 26 that begins "If you're headed" is from Robert F. Cross, *Sailor in the White House: The Seafaring Life of FDR* (Annapolis: Naval Institute Press, 2003), epigraph, n.p.

The *New York Times* article reproduced on page 26 is "F. D. Roosevelt Buys Spa" (*New York Times*, April 26, 1926).

The quotation by Louis Howe on page 27 is from Julie M. Fenster, *FDR's Shadow: Louis Howe, the Force that Shaped Franklin and Eleanor Roosevelt* (New York: Palgrave Macmillan, 2009), 189.

FDR's dedication to Lucy Mercer on page 28 is from Joseph E. Persico, *Franklin and Lucy: Mrs. Rutherfurd and Other Remarkable Women in Roosevelt's Life* (New York: Random House, 2009), 179.

The quotation from James Roosevelt on page 28 is from James Roosevelt, *My Parents: A Differing View* (Chicago: Playboy Press, 1976), 93.

"Learning to Shoot"

The definition of sensei on page 95 quotes Sensei Mitch, "What Is a Sensei," Martial Thoughts, https://karatetraining.org/weblog/what-is-a-sensei/#gsc.tab=0, accessed September 3, 2023.

Acknowledgments

Grateful acknowledgment is made to the publications where these essays first appeared, often in different versions:

The Common: "Jamali Kamali Airborne in History"

Gargoyle: "Hedgeballs and Rinkydinks" (as "Oedipus in the Backseat")

Journal of Poetry Therapy: "A Poet's Job on the Ward"

Southwest Review: "Learning to Shoot"

upstreet number eleven: "Befriend Only to Betray"

"Learning to Shoot" was cited in *Best American Essays* 2004, edited by Robert Atwan (Boston, MA: Houghton Mifflin Harcourt, 2004).

"BOOM: A Vaccine Story" and "Polio Boulevard" appeared in the book *Polio Boulevard* (State University of New York Press, 2014). "Ship Ahoy: FDR's Houseboat Years" appeared in the book *FDR on his Houseboat: The Larooco Log, 1924–1926* (State University of New York Press, 2016).

"A Poet's Job on the Ward" was reprinted in the book *Land of Stone: Breaking Silence Through Poetry* (Wayne State University Press, 2007).

CavanKerry's Mission

A not-for-profit literary press serving art and community,
CavanKerry is committed to expanding the reach of poetry and
other fine literature to a general readership by publishing works
that explore the emotional and psychological landscapes of
everyday life, and to bringing that art to the underserved where
they live, work, and receive services.

Other Prose Collections from CavanKerry Press

Italian Blood: A Memoir, Denise Tolan

Unnatural Selection: A Memoir of Wilderness and Adoption,
Andrea Ross

Truth Has a Different Shape, Kari L. O'Driscoll

My Mother's Funeral, Adriana Páramo

Primary Lessons, Sarah Bracey White

Confessions of Joan the Tall, Joan Cusack Handler

Motherhood Exaggerated, Judith Hannan

Letters From a Distant Shore, Marie Lawson Fiala

The Poetry Life Ten Stories, Baron Wormser

To The Marrow, Robert Seder

The Gradual Twilight: An appreciation of John Haines,
Ed. Steven B. Rogers

Carolyn Kizer: Perspectives on Her Life & Work,
Ed. Finch, Keller, McClelland

This book was printed on paper from responsible sources.

History Is Embarrassing was typeset in Chaparral Pro,
created by Carol Twombly in 2000 for Adobe. Its design was
inspired by the roman book lettering of the sixteenth century
and the slab serifs of the nineteenth.